I0788719

The Complication

By:

John Hagen

The Complication

Copyright © 2024

Dedication

To my wonderful wife, Ileana. You light up my life with love and understanding.

Acknowledgment

This is a work of fiction. All the characters, places, and events described in this novel are from the author's imagination, or the author has used them fictitiously. Some ideas in the novel stemmed from actual events. One cold and wet December evening at dinner, my friend and colleague Allan told an engaging story. I have fictionalized part of what he told me and embedded it in the story. The rest is from my imagination.

Contents

About the Author

John Hagen is a retired laparoscopic surgeon living in Toronto. Working in a large community teaching hospital, he was chief of surgery and then chief of staff before retiring from surgical practice. As a passionate sailor, he spent one winter season in the Bahamas and another in the Caribbean. He spends the summers sailing on Lake Ontario from his home port of Port Credit.

Chapter 1

The ambulance had the lights flashing, and the siren blared at the maximum volume. The paramedics had a true emergency transfer on their hands. They were barreling along the city streets at 80 km/h, swerving around stopped cars to blast through the red lights. Although it was 8 AM on Saturday, the streets of Toronto had many cars. Some drivers were on their way to work, and others were returning after a night of parties as the Toronto Film Festival was in full swing. A surgeon sat beside the patient, pumping saline solution into the wide-bore intravenous line as the ambulance bounced up and down on the uneven pavement. It would take 20 minutes to get to the tertiary care hospital, and in the first 5 minutes, he had already administered 2 liters of the life-saving solution. The blood pressure was still low at 70/30, and the heart rate was 130 beats per minute.

There were two paramedics on board. One was driving the ambulance; the other was ventilating the unconscious patient. John Hegland, the surgeon resuscitating the unstable patient, looked up at the paramedic who was ventilating with an Ambu bag and shook his head. The paramedic simply shrugged. For him, this was just another transfer. The surgeon knew this would be a life-altering event for him, and he was already preparing for the fallout. He wondered how it was possible for things to spin out of control so quickly.

The Complication

John Hegland was the acting chief of surgery at a large community hospital in the northwest section of Toronto. John was 37 years old. This was his 7th year as a staff surgeon. He was tall and was physically fit from running. Running the Ottawa marathon this past spring was a highlight for him. John was training for the waterfront marathon, which would be in a few weeks. He had short brown hair and a handsome face.

Earlier that morning, his surgical confidence shone through as he walked from room to room on the surgical floor, making rounds early on a Saturday morning. One of the new nursing recruits, Shirley, accompanied him, taking notes as they discussed each patient's care plan. Shirley was pushing a cart that contained the patients' records in marked slots. They clipped the new lab results on the front of the charts to be signed off.

John was on call for the weekend, meaning he would see all the patients his 13 other colleagues were looking after during the week. On weekends, they transferred the patients' care to the on-call surgeon so that the others could rest and recuperate after a busy week of surgery.

Turning to Shirley, John asked, "Who's next on our list?"

"The next one is in room 508," replied Shirley. "A laparoscopic cholecystectomy from yesterday. I'm a little worried about him. He's having more pain than usual."

"Let's look at the lab work from this morning," said John. He reached down and pulled up the chart. They highlighted the abnormal results in red. At first glance, the abnormal red highlights covered the sheet. The AST levels were 15,000, and the bilirubin was 100. The white blood count was 30,000.

"What?" John blurted out. "These levels are grossly abnormal. I've seen nothing like this before. There must be a mistake!"

Shirley looked at the paper and said, "It's today's date, and they drew the blood at 6:10 AM. The name is Brian Feldman, and he's in 508."

"Ok, let's look at him," said John.

Upon entering the room, a woman sitting in the chair bolted to a standing position. She spoke at a rapid pace that was difficult to follow. "I'm the daughter, Miriam. There's something wrong with my dad. I knew I should never have brought him to this shitty hospital. Dr. Sawchuck said it was a minor surgery, and he wouldn't have to stay in the hospital, but he had a terrible night. What the hell is going on here? How come you didn't come in to see him last night?" She burst into tears.

John stopped and listened to her. When she started to cry and stopped speaking, John said softly, "I'm sorry he had a rough night.

Let me examine him, and we can have a discussion. Shirley, can you take Miriam into the waiting room and bring her a coffee or a drink? I'll be there in a few minutes."

Shirley left the room with Miriam. He could hear her sobbing as Shirley walked down the hall into the waiting room. The nurses had attached Brian Feldman to the monitors. His pulse rate was 120, and his blood pressure was 110/70. His breathing was rapid and shallow. John observed that the whites of Brian Feldman's eyes were jaundiced.

"Mr. Feldman, my name is Dr. Hegland. I'm on call for surgery today, so I'll be looking after you. Are you in any pain?"

Brian rolled his eyes towards John, then closed them.

"Is it alright if I examine you?" asked John. There was no response from Brian.

"I'm going to pull back the sheet and examine your abdomen," said John.

John pulled back the bedsheet. There was a dressing covering the abdomen, which he removed. It surprised him to see a large incision running down the right side of the abdomen just below the ribs. This was supposed to be a laparoscopic cholecystectomy, he thought. John palpated the abdomen, causing Brian to wince in pain. Gently shaking the bed resulted in a whimper from Brian. John looked at the incision, which seemed a little swollen. He removed the steristrips on the edge of the incision. A large gush of green fluid under pressure escaped, covering his gloved hands. He gently put his index finger in the incision, which released about a liter of green fluid soaking the bedsheets. John placed the dressing over the incision and covered Brian's abdomen with the bedsheet.

John removed his gloves and washed his hands. He took a deep breath. This wasn't good. Bile leaking out from an incision 1-day post-op could only mean one thing. There must be a serious bile duct injury. He told himself I'd better call Dr. Sawchuck and find out what happened. John walked to the nursing station and reviewed the chart. There was no mention of any problem at the time of surgery. No notes described what had happened. Typically, the dictated operative note would not appear on the chart for 2-3 days.

"Joe," said John after dialing Dr. Sawchuk's number. "I'm on call for the weekend and making rounds. Could you tell me about Brian Feldman?"

"John, you're on call for the weekend. You figure it out. You have no right to bother me on my weekend off," retorted Joe.

"Yeh, sorry to bother you," said John. "But no notes are describing what happened at the surgery. There's a large incision."

"It was a difficult cholecystectomy, so I converted to a laparotomy and removed the gallbladder that way," said Joe, raising his voice. "Now that is not so complicated, is it? You should be able to figure all that out yourself. Now leave me alone." John heard the phone disconnect.

"I guess I am alone," John said to the disconnected phone.

John walked down the hall to the waiting room and sat beside Miriam. "Can we talk about your dad?" asked John.

Miriam nodded her head. "It's bad, isn't it?"

"Well, I'm not sure yet," said John. "We are getting a portable ultrasound to see if there is any fluid in his abdomen, but I am concerned that there has been a complication. One thing that we worry about with gallbladder surgery is common bile duct injury." On a napkin, John drew a diagram illustrating the anatomy and highlighted the potential injury to the common bile duct. "It is a known risk with this kind of surgery."

"Where is the surgeon, Dr. Sawchuk?" asked Miriam. "I want to speak with that asshole."

"I spoke with him this morning to find out if there were any problems at the surgery. He told me it was straightforward, although a little difficult," said John. "They are doing the ultrasound now, so how about if we talk in 15 minutes after I have reviewed it?"

"What will you do if there is a bile duct injury?" asked Miriam.

"I'm going to arrange a transfer to a downtown hospital where they have a hepatobiliary service," said John. "Your dad will require another operation to fix the problem."

"Oh my God!" cried out Miriam. "What a terrible nightmare. This is the worst hospital. This is all your fault. You should have come into the hospital to see him last night."

John sighed. "I'm sorry about this. I'm going to begin arrangements to have him transferred."

John walked back to the nursing station. He called his friend and colleague at the main downtown hospital. "Paul, I have a problem that I hope you can help me with," said John. "This morning, I saw a patient who was jaundiced and had bile flowing out of his laparotomy incision one day after an open cholecystectomy. The ultrasound shows free fluid, but more alarming, there does not appear to be blood flowing to the right lobe of the liver."

Paul was quiet on the other end of the phone. "We have no beds, but this sounds serious. Can you organize a transfer to the emergency room? I'll deal with the wrath of the bed co-ordinator when the patient gets here. Once here, we will look after him."

"I'm going to come with him in the ambulance," said John. "I think he'll need to be intubated and ventilated before we leave. Another thing. The family is quite upset. I think they will create trouble for us, so be careful how you talk with them."

John went to the waiting room to talk to Miriam. There were 2 men in the room, Brian Feldman's sons, Rick and Remo, with Miriam. They were both huge. They were in their 20s and had large muscles bulging through their t-shirts.

"Are you the asshole responsible for fucking up my dad?" said Rick, the larger of the two.

Before John could answer, he grabbed John by the shirt and rammed him against the wall. John's head slammed into the drywall, making a dent from the force. Pain shot through the back of John's skull, and he saw stars before collapsing on the floor when the brother released him.

"Asshole!" Rick muttered as he kicked John in the stomach and walked out of the door. Miriam and the other brother followed him. They walked to the end of the hall, down the stairs and out the fire exit into the parking lot.

Shirley, who walked into the room just as John hit the floor, ran out of the room and down the hall to the nursing station, screaming at the top of her lungs. The security team arrived within

30 seconds and helped John to sit on a chair. "You need to go to the emergency room," said one of them.

John brushed them off. "I need to look after the patient," said John. With that, he limped out of the waiting room and into room 508 to help get Brian Feldman ready to be transferred downtown.

Chapter 2

The members of the medical advisor committee were listening to the chief of staff. They were in the hospital's boardroom. It was 6 PM on a Thursday in early November. It was already dark outside. The light cast from the windows revealed that the strong, icy, cold, northerly winds were blowing the falling snow horizontally. Inside the boardroom, the conversation was icy as well.

"The question I have for you, Dr. Hegland, is why have you allowed Dr. Sawchuk to continue to practice at our hospital?" asked Nigel Gilman, the chief of staff.

All eyes of the medical advisory committee fixated on John Hegland. The committee comprised the department chiefs and medical staff association executives. They ensured that the quality of care was of the highest standard possible at the hospital. John reluctantly accepted the position of chief of surgery after the previous chief left suddenly. They gave him the status of 'acting chief of surgery' until a selection committee could convene to interview a surgeon for the position. John had no leadership training or experience, so he relied on intuition and common sense.

"Let me start by saying I was also involved with this case," responded John. "I helped transport the patient to the hepatobiliary center and was present when he went for the second operation downtown. They found that Dr. Sawchuk had resected the common bile duct to the hepatic plate. He ligated the right hepatic artery, making the right lobe of the liver infarct. Paul performed a massive liver resection to remove the infarcted right lobe of the liver. A bile duct reconstruction was difficult. Because the remaining bile ducts were 2 mm in diameter, the anastomosis to the limb of the small intestine was very difficult."

"The family has gone to the press," said Nigel. "They want to know how we are managing this surgical incompetence. They both want to know why no one has suspended him. I am asking you the same question."

"None of you in the room except me are surgeons," said John. "Complications govern a surgeon's life. If we suspended a surgeon every time there was a complication, there would be none of us left to do surgery. As members of the medical advisory committee, you should be asking what we can do to help Joe through this difficult time rather than what we can do to punish him."

The room went silent. Nigel's face went red. "I knew it was a mistake taking you on as acting chief of surgery. You have no experience in dealing with these kinds of issues. Grow a pair of balls and tell him you suspend him while investigating. The board wants to know how we are managing the press. Given your left-leaning opinions, please do not speak with the press."

John glared at Nigel. This was not the first time they had disagreed. This was the first time Nigel had admonished him publicly. "You are in no position to comment on what is appropriate for a surgeon. You have no right to humiliate me in front of my colleagues. As the chief of staff, I expect you to monitor your emotions. I would be happy to discuss the comments you made about my inexperience with you privately. To say something like that in front of my colleagues was inappropriate and hurtful. I think you are the one who needs to improve your leadership skills."

John stood up and said, "I am leaving this meeting. I would be happy to reconvene after an agreement to discuss the issue with civility."

John closed his laptop and headed out of the door. The room remained dead silent.

John felt his pulse racing. It felt like a vice grip clenched his guts in the pit of his stomach. He felt his face was flushed. The breathing was rapid and shallow as he paced the floor. He had never felt so demeaned in his life. John hesitated to take on the role of chief when they initially approached him. He was new on staff and recognized he needed to take some leadership courses to be an effective chief. For Nigel Gilman to focus on his insecurities and what John knew were his weaknesses was doubly frustrating. John paced in the hallway outside his chief of surgery office. There was no one else around, as it was after hours. The cleaning staff had already finished their duties, so the hallway was empty. John always thought more clearly when he was on the move. A thought came to his mind. He would call his mentor, Bennie Langford, for advice. He was the chief of surgery for the University of Toronto. Bennie would know what to do.

When John was a resident, 7 years earlier, Bennie was the staff he feared most. His nickname from the residents behind his back was 'Eagle Eyes' because he never seemed to miss any minor detail. He expected the same from the residents. For six months on Bennie's rotation, John was on his toes. John would be the first on the floor every morning to review the x-rays and lab work before Bennie arrived. He would make sure there was a solid management plan for each patient. Bennie was a shrewd judge of character. He could tell when you were not being truthful. Often, he would ask about a lab result when he knew the answer just to see if you did as well. Bennie had ended more than one resident's career when he caught them making up information, trying to impress him. Even to this day, John would get a flash of anxiety running through his gut when he thought about speaking with Bennie.

John dialed Bennie's cell phone. Bennie answered on the third ring.

"I was hoping you could advise me?" asked John.

John described the surgical complication that Brian Feldman sustained and the subsequent surgery. "Have you ever seen a complication as bad as that?" asked John.

Bennie, never one for many words, was quiet for a moment. "I have seen much worse than that," he said.

"What should I do? The chief of staff says I must suspend him pending an investigation," said John.

Bennie explained, "As chief of surgery, your responsibilities include investigating the incident. Only the medical advisory committee can decide on suspension. I suspect the chief of staff would not have enough votes to effect a suspension; therefore, he was hard on you. He wanted you to carry out his dirty work so that he could inform the board about the suspension of the surgeon. I agree with you; Dr. Sawchuk needs to be supported. From what you are saying, he has been a surgeon on staff there for 25 years and has an outstanding record."

"Err…" said John. "About 3 years ago, I was doing a case with him at night. He smelled of alcohol. I suggested transferring the case to me, but he brushed me off, saying he was fine. As a junior staff member, I didn't want to make any waves, so I just talked with him after he finished the case. I said if I suspected alcohol use with him again, I would tell the chief of staff and let him deal with it. I think I made an impact because about 2 weeks later, he went on medical leave for 6 months to treat alcoholism. Within a year of returning, he was back to full-time.

"Two days ago, with Joe's permission, I called his rehab physician, Dr. Graham Lewis, and asked him if he had any concerns about relapse. Graham told me in no uncertain terms that Joe was not drinking. He described the rehab program, the negative urine screens, and his attendance at the AA meetings. Graham said that Joe was a model for reformed alcoholics and an inspiration for others. He also said that Joe had discussed the case with his group, and support was in place to help him get through this difficult time. We had rounds at our division meeting and discussed the case. A list resulted in recommendations that we all agreed upon. We also recommended calling for help if the surgeon contemplated conversion to a laparotomy."

Bennie went quiet again. "As chief, you must meet with Joe at least once a month and carefully note the encounters. Your role should focus on helping him and identifying any patient safety concerns. You must also find a way to get along with your chief of staff; otherwise, he could make your life miserable."

John thought about this for a few seconds before responding. "Again, you have given me very sage advice. Thank you. Would you be okay if I call you again for more advice?"

"No problem," was the response. The phone call ended. John breathed a sigh of relief. He had done the right thing by standing up to the chief of staff. His anxiety settled as he walked out of the hospital.

John walked to the parking lot and hopped in the car. He stopped at a local pizza place and picked up a pizza to take home. The TV was on the news station. John's jaw dropped when his face appeared on the screen. Underneath his picture was the caption, "Chief of surgery allows the surgeon to operate while drunk."

Chapter 3

Nigel Gilman lay awake. It was 2 AM. He was thinking about the disastrous medical advisory committee meeting. Underestimating that shit, John Hegland, was something he could not get out of his mind. He had big plans and was on track to be the province's next Deputy Minister of Health. He needed this incident involving this terrible complication to go away. Nigel had come this far and would not let some incompetent surgeon and his equally incompetent chief derail his plans. The news interview earlier in the day was equally disastrous.

"There's a TV reporter, Ashley, here to see you," Anita, Nigel's assistant, said to Nigel over the intercom. It was 10 AM and Nigel was sitting in his office reviewing the previous Medical Advisory Committee meeting's minutes. He was good with reporter interviews because he could think quickly and was skilled at controlling the content of the conversation. He believed any publicity involving getting his face on the 6 o'clock news was good publicity.

"Send her in," said Nigel. He stood up from his desk and opened his door to let the reporter and her team into his office. Ashley walked in with the confidence that comes after years of news reporting and thousands of interviews. She was blonde with wavy hair. Not a single strand was out of place. Her makeup was perfect for the incandescent light of the office. She felt beautiful and powerful in her mid-thigh skirt and white blouse, outlining her perfect shape. She smiled at Nigel, and he smiled back.

"Are you OK if we set up the camera beside the Peloton machine?" asked Ashley. "You can sit at your desk, and I'll sit across from you."

"That sounds good," said Nigel. Ashley explained they had questions about the case that they transferred to the hepatobiliary center while the crew set up the cameras. Ashley revealed how grateful she was to talk with him by complimenting him on his chief of staff position and how lucky the hospital was to have him.

"Ready to go live in three, two, one," counted Ashley. "I'm with Nigel Gilman, the chief of staff. Thank you for meeting with me. We are discussing the patient transferred from your hospital to the hepatobiliary center. I understand you have launched an investigation."

"Yes," responded Nigel. "We review any serious complication to determine why it occurred and what we can do to prevent it from happening again."

"We spoke with Dr. Sawchuk's ex-wife," said Ashley. "She says that he had a drinking problem. The current chief of surgery, Dr. John Hegland, allowed him to operate on a patient after he had been drinking. How do you know he has not continued to drink?"

Nigel was at a loss for words. This was not what he was expecting. His mind was reeling, trying to find a way out of this downward spiral the interview was heading for. He looked directly at Ashley and said, "That happened before I became chief of staff. I would never have let him operate again. Our current chief of surgery is only holding the position temporarily until we can find someone more suited to the position."

"Are you allowing Dr. Sawchuk to operate now?" asked Ashley.

Nigel's face went red. "That is under review," he responded. "I cannot say anything more about it because the investigation is still ongoing."

"Thank you, Dr. Gilman," said Ashley. "Now, back to the studio for an update on the traffic."

Nigel glared at Ashley. "You sandbagged me," he said.

Ashley said, "Thanks for the interview. You did great." She exited the chair and walked out the door down the hallway before Nigel said anything else.

Nigel scored the highest marks in his class when he graduated from medical school at the University of Toronto 20 years ago. Harvard, Yale, and the Mayo Clinic were competing for him to be their star resident in internal medicine. He chose Harvard mainly because of their reputation for placing their graduates in the highest-paying jobs. Nigel completed 4 years of internal medicine training, followed by 2 years of nephrology. He had a dozen publications as the primary author, two of which were in the Lancet, one of the top-ranked medical journals in the world. He entertained top job offers across North America but chose the University of Toronto. They gave him the best offer. He was the division head of nephrology and then the chief of medicine at Toronto General Hospital, the highest-rated hospital in Canada.

Nigel was tall and thin. Although he liked to exercise, he had knee problems and could no longer run. He set up a Peloton in his hospital office. He had the IT team fix a computer on the handles of the stationary exercise bicycle so he could perform exercises while answering emails. Nigel used his tall frame to tower over those smaller than him in an intimidating manner. It was easy for him because 90% of the administrative staff at the hospital were women. He believed fervently they were not as smart as he was. He found them easy to manipulate.

The chief of staff position at the largest community hospital in Toronto was going to be his stepping stone to greater positions. After 3 interviews, they selected him. That was 2 years ago. In his mind, they were lucky to have him. He could feel all eyes on him as he paraded around the hospital. When he spoke at the many administrative meetings, the room would go quiet, and the people in the room would hang on to his every word. If someone attempted to slip in a dissenting opinion, he would shut them down before they got their point across. He knew how to play on their insecurities. Public humiliation would stop anyone from disagreeing with him.

He did not understand how his tactics had failed him at the medical advisory meeting. Never had a subordinate challenged his leadership style in public and then walked out of the meeting before he put them back in their place. He would not let that happen again. The chair of the board of directors had called him after the Medical Advisory meeting, asking him how he was going to make the publicity crisis go away. Nigel needed this negative press to disappear if he wanted to advance his career.

"What's the matter, honey?" said the woman lying next to him he thought was asleep.

Rebecca, a beautiful woman, was of Chinese origin and had arrived in Canada with her parents 30 years earlier. They had fled the grip of communist China and arrived with only the clothes on their backs. Her father had worked in a dry-cleaning store until he had saved enough to start one for himself. He worked 16 hours a day. His single goal was to provide a better life for his only child, Rebecca.

Rebecca had long black hair that went almost to her waist. Her eyes would shine when she laughed, and small dimples would appear on the side of her mouth. Her round face possessed the beauty only seen in Orientals. Although she was 39 years old, her youthfulness could allow her to pass for 25. Yoga and Pilates kept her trim body fit. She had unbelievable flexibility. As an example, she would show off by resting her hands flat on the floor when she bent over. She would then bring her head and shoulders between her thighs, contorting herself in an impossible position. Lowering herself to the floor, she would twist herself like a pretzel so an arm would appear where it should have been a leg. Nigel told her that this was something that turned him on. She suspected others felt the same way.

Rebecca was the assistant to the current Deputy Minister of Health. They chose her from a list of 40 equally eligible candidates, largely because of her Chinese ethnicity. Employment equity was high on the list of government priorities. Her high intelligence and beauty were secondary, but helpful in her position. She had been at the job for the past 6 months. She had been discussing with Nigel how her current boss had made some major mistakes, and they would probably terminate him in the next few months. This would open the opportunity for Nigel to apply for the position. With her on the inside, she would make sure it would happen. When it came to getting what she wanted, Rebecca was ruthless.

"I need to make the terrible publicity go away," said Nigel. "Unless I do something drastic, I will come across as a weak leader. The mistaken perception will be that I cannot effectively manage my staff of surgeons. No one will hire a weak leader in the position of Deputy Minister of Health."

Rebecca was quiet. Nigel sat up in bed and turned to her. "This is the opportunity of a lifetime. Not only would my salary double to $800,000 per year, but I would also have control of the multibillion-dollar healthcare budget. Pharmacare companies will pay handsomely to get their hands on those provincial drug care contracts. If we are careful, we will be richer than ever imagined. To think that a drunk surgeon and his weak chief place that in jeopardy is a travesty."

"I can fix this for you," said Rebecca quietly.

"How?" asked Nigel incredulously.

Rebecca hesitated before answering. There would be no going back. She, too, needed Nigel as the Deputy Minister of Health if she wanted to improve her life. Life in China over the past 30 years has improved for the Chinese. Once her business plan in Canada was put into action, she thought about moving back to China. She had a thriving business there but needed better access to information from the province's database to take her business to the next level. Only with Nigel at the helm would that be possible.

"You don't want to know," said Rebecca. She turned to him and kissed him on the mouth. She slipped her tongue inside and, with her hand, rubbed his crotch.

As Nigel became aroused, she lay on her back and spread her legs. She said, "Send me $20,000, and in one week, your troubles will be over."

Chapter 4

John was standing in a lecture hall in a 2000-bed hospital in Yangzhou, China, in front of 400 surgeons. He had just finished giving a lecture on the value of using an intravenous compound called ICG when performing an anastomosis. After a bowel resection, the biggest fear among surgeons is anastomotic leakage. When a leak occurs, sepsis and even death can follow. John was showing the results of an extensive study, confirming reduced leak rates after the ICG administration. If the ICG confirmed that the blood supply to the anastomosis was excellent, there were fewer leaks.

"Great presentation!" said Hong, the surgeon who had invited him. "I'm glad that the president of the hospital was here today. We are going to have to upgrade our laparoscopic equipment to do this. It means more money, but if it reduces our leak rate, I can make an argument our overall costs will be less."

Although communist principles founded modern China, patients had to pay for their health care. Unlike Canada, where the government pays for all health care costs, in China, they pass all costs on to the patients. The expectation of the Chinese patients was perfection. There was little tolerance for any complication that might arise.

The Complication

"We would like to present a complex patient management case if you are okay with that," suggested Hong.

"I am happy to do this," answered John.

Hong and John walked to the elevator and up to the 15th floor, the general surgery floor. They entered a small conference room. There were about 10 staff surgeons and 10 trainees sitting around an oval table. At the front of the room was a large monitor with a PowerPoint presentation. The words on the PowerPoint were in English, but the trainee presenting the case spoke in Mandarin. The case was that of a 55-year-old man who had a laparoscopic sigmoid colon resection for a carcinoma. On post-op day 3, tachycardia developed, and they suspected anastomotic leakage. Diagnostic laparoscopy confirmed a leak at the anastomosis, and they inserted drains. A loop ileostomy bypassed the stool into a bag to allow the leak to heal. The plan was to close the ileostomy once the leak healed in 2 or 3 months. The problem was there was a constant flow of blood and infection from the rectum, and the patient remained septic. A CAT scan-guided drainage insertion into the presacral space failed to control the sepsis.

After he asked a few questions, John suggested, "I would recommend taking the patient back to the operating room and get better drainage. He may require a laparotomy."

The Complication

The room was silent. The staff surgeons looked at each other. Hong's eyes darted around the room. His right leg moved up and down on the floor in a nervous, erratic motion. A twitch developed on the right side of his face. He began to say something, then stopped. After 10 seconds, he could speak.

"Would you help us?" asked Hong. "We could have him ready for surgery in less than an hour."

John nodded in affirmation.

The operating room was on the 2nd floor. Hong and John went there together, got changed into scrub suits and went into OR 10, the general surgery room. By the time they got there, the anesthesiologist had intubated the patient, and the patient was asleep. The two surgeons scrubbed at the sink and dried their hands, and the nurse helped tie up their surgical gowns. They were standing across from one another when Hong passed the scalpel to John.

"I thought I was going to help you," stated John.

"Please go ahead. There is much you can teach us," said Hong. "The rest of the surgeons are in the conference room, and they connected us on a video feed. They want to see you operate."

John smiled. This was not what he was expecting, but as a guest, he would not argue. A thought passed through his mind. His malpractice insurance only covered him when he worked in Canada.

Perhaps this hospital had its liability coverage, which would include him as a guest surgeon. It was too late to explore this as a possibility, as the knife was already in his hand.

"We'll start with the laparoscope to see if we can access the abscess that way," said John to the group of surgeons in the conference room.

John opened the small umbilical incision and inserted the laparoscope. The video image showed adhesions plastered on the small intestine to the pelvis. It would not be safe to proceed laparoscopically, and John told this to the crowd of surgeons using the video feed. John removed the laparoscope. He made a large incision from the pubis to above the umbilicus. He placed the retractors to hold the incision open. Using gentle dissection with his fingers, John pulled the small intestine out of the pelvis. Using his fingers, John probed the space in front of the sacrum and entered a large abscess with thick pus. After washing the space with a saline solution, he placed 2 drains and brought them through the skin on the right side of the incision.

"I think we should bring out the anastomosis, as this is the source of the infection," explained John. He made a small circular incision in the left side of the abdomen and brought out the anastomosis as a stoma.

After the surgery had finished, Hong took John to the restaurant that was in the hospital. They sat down after Hong ordered food for them.

"There's something else I should have told you," said Hong sheepishly. "It was the family that requested you do the surgery. In China, there is the belief that North American surgeons are better than those in China."

"I am flattered," said John. "But I have not found that to be the case. In China, you have such large volumes of cases, you get very good at laparoscopic techniques."

"Another thing," said Hong. "The last surgeon who operated on this patient was murdered."

John, who had just taken a sip of tea, choked and began coughing. "What," he cried. After the coughing stopped, he blurted out, "What happened?"

"The family was angry with the surgeon because of the anastomotic leak," explained Hong. "They said he did not do the operation correctly, and that is why he leaked. The surgeon warned them about the possibility of leakage before the surgery, but when it occurred, it came as a shock to them. They started hitting him in the waiting room when he told them about the findings after the second operation."

"Did he call the police?" asked John.

"The police will do nothing and will only further aggravate the family," said Hong. "This happens all the time in China. The family will beat up the doctors if things do not go well after an operation. Usually, that is all that happens. The surgeon takes his beating and then gets back to work. A few days ago, he did not turn up for work. The security team from the hospital went to his apartment. They found him dead. The assumption was that he slipped in the bathroom while having a shower. An autopsy found that someone had strangled him. Someone had crushed the larynx. The only explanation was that the angry family was responsible. The police investigation determined the family was out of the city at the time of death. They have charged no one for the murder."

John went quiet. He thought back to his own experience at his hospital in Toronto. There was an exchange program where John would send residents to China, and Chinese surgeons would visit John for 3 months. They could not perform surgery, or help with patient care because of licensing restrictions, but could observe any operation. One night, when John was on call, he went to visit a patient on the surgical floor. He brought Gong, a surgeon visiting from Guangzhou, to see the patient. It was a 50-year-old woman who had a laparoscopic colon resection the day before by Dr. Shier, one of the general surgeons. She now had a fever of 39 degrees and peritonitis. Gong agreed with John that the patient needed to go back to the operating room. At surgery, there was a tear in the small intestine, likely from the surgical graspers. John sutured the tear and washed out the abdomen.

After the surgery, John took Gong with him when he talked with the patient's family. He told the patient's family that the inadvertent enterotomy was likely a result of accidentally tearing the small bowel with an instrument. John pointed out that this was a known risk of laparoscopic surgery. John told them to expect a speedy recovery. Gong listened incredulously as John explained this to the family. Even more surprising to Gong was when the family thanked John for giving such excellent care.

As they were walking back to the surgeon's lounge, Gong said, "In China, they would hit you. No surgeon would take another surgeon's patient back to the operating room for fear of being blamed for the complication. Last year in China, unhappy patients or their families murdered 500 doctors following bad outcomes. You practice in an alternate universe where they thank you for your help. You do not know how lucky you are."

As John thought back on this conversation, he developed the familiar tightness in his chest that he experienced when anxiety took over. Now that John knew that someone had murdered the last surgeon who operated on the patient, he asked, "Am I in any danger?"

"Absolutely not," replied Hong. "The family was most appreciative that we could fly in the best surgeon in Toronto to fix the problem. You have nothing to worry about. If anything goes wrong, it is me they will blame. As you have taught me in the past when I visited you in Toronto, I am keeping my fingers crossed…..."

Wow, thought John. I truly am lucky to live in Canada.

Chapter 5

The icy wind was blowing from the west. Lake Ontario would get strong winds in the fall before the winter storms arrived. There was some protection from the wind and waves from the dodger that was protecting the cockpit of the 35-foot sailboat. It was dusk as the sailboat approached the finish line. All seven crew members sat on the windward rail as a counterweight to keep the boat from heeling too much from the strong wind. John Hegland was at the helm of his racing sailboat. It was the Wednesday night race, and the season was almost over. This was the last race of the year before the winter arrived. Their chief competition, a boat named Rhumbline, had just crossed the finish line ahead of them. There was still a chance John could beat them. All boats had a handicap rating. As John had a slower boat, his rating allowed him an extra 10 seconds every mile over Rhumbline. John glanced at his watch. He had to cross the finish line in the next 40 seconds to beat them. They were at least a minute away. John sighed. The crew would feel disappointed.

Racing his sailboat was a way of relieving stress. For John, he was not so much interested in winning. Just being on the water caused the worries of his surgical practice and his failing marriage to melt away. It felt like the wind blew away all the troubles. The camaraderie of the crew before the race and the beer drinking while sitting in the cockpit after the race were the warm comforts he looked forward to. He knew he would miss the weekly racing when they hauled out the boat to store for the winter.

John thought back on today's race. The start was exciting; they were the first ones across the start line. There was no one upwind of them, so they had undisturbed wind filling their sails. This was not the case for their chief competition, Rhumbline. By careful maneuvering, they had their competition pinned in a position downwind of them. The disturbed airflow in their sails prevented them from powering past John's boat, which was slightly slower. They were ahead of Rhumbline when they reached the windward mark. Launching the spinnaker for the downwind leg went flawlessly. However, Rhumbline positioned themselves to deliver disturbed air into John's sails. This tactic allowed Rhumbline to power past John. When they arrived at the leeward mark, Rhumbline was four boat lengths ahead of them. John's crew hoisted the jib just ahead of dousing the spinnaker, while John steered the sailboat upwind. The crew positioned themselves on the windward rail to balance the boat's weight. Suzie, the foredeck person, left the foredeck and went into the boat's cabin to pack the spinnaker so it would be ready for the next downwind leg. They had sailed perfectly for the rest of the race, but they could not catch up to Rhumbline.

Suzie was in her late twenties and had thick black hair tied up. She worked as a schoolteacher and was downtown Toronto's psychologist. A sparkle in her eye lit up her pretty face whenever the subject of sailing came up. Suzie loved being on the water. Her small size and light weight made her excellent in her current crewing position. She had the perfect body type for the foredeck position because she was light and quick. There was another reason she loved sailing on John's boat. She had a huge crush on him. There was some talk of trouble in his marriage, but she did not know the details. She would wait patiently and be ready if John was interested in her.

John steered the boat over the finish line. The committee boat blasted the horn, which indicated the time of the finish. Gerry, the chief tactician, glanced at his watch.

"We are 55 seconds behind Rhumbline," said Gerry. "After correcting for the handicap, they only beat us by 15 seconds tonight. That was one of the best races of the season! I think we will get a second-place finish tonight!"

"Whoo hoo!" hooted the rest of the crew in unison. They hopped up from their positions on the rail as the race was over and prepared to take down the sails. John headed the boat into the wind, and the crew pulled down the jib and lashed it onto the deck. John started the engine to keep the boat in the wind so the mainsail could come down. The boat bounced gently against the waves and wind as the crew lowered the mainsail and lashed it to the boom. They had done this so many times over the season, the routine was flawless. John steered his sailboat toward the dock.

Later, as they sat in the cockpit, drinking beer and munching on potato chips, the conversation bounced around about the race. Gerry complimented the crew on the spinnaker takedown, which had always slowed the boat down in other races. Tonight, they perfectly executed the takedown, as Suzie was the foredeck person. That was largely her job. She smiled at the compliment.

As the conversation died, Suzie asked John, "Was that you I saw on the news last week? What was that about?"

The rest of the crew went quiet. John said, "Well, you can't believe everything you hear on the news. I'm in the lucky position of acting chief of surgery, so if there is any bad press, I am their first target. Fortunately, the press is onto bigger news items now. I am hoping they have forgotten about me."

The crew laughed nervously. "We worry about you, John. You need to take care of yourself," said Suzie.

"I'm doing OK. It was a great season with you as my crew. I'm going to miss all of this," said John solemnly. "Look, I've got a 46-foot Beneteau booked for the second week of December in Antigua. If any of you want to come, you are welcome. We can split the cost of food. The boat will cost $8000. It can accommodate 3 couples. Maybe you can think about it and let me know. I'll email everyone."

John looked at his watch. "I better get a move on," he said.

They said their goodbyes and promised to get together for a wing night in the winter. John was the last one off the boat. He locked the boat and stepped onto the dock. It was dark, but there was light from the power station where John plugged the electric cord. The power would keep the batteries charged and keep the fridge going.

"Hey asshole," said a voice. He was standing next to the power station. John stopped in his tracks. It was the same man who had smashed his head into the drywall: Rick, the son of Brian Feldman. He was holding what appeared to be a short club in his right hand, gently hitting the palm of his left hand. He was wearing a black hoodie and a black tracksuit. John's boat was at the end of the dock, the farthest from the clubhouse. This man was the only other person on the dock. To get to the clubhouse, John would have to get past him. The man was blocking the way.

"I'm going to pound you until you get some sense," the man with the club said. "They didn't pay me enough to kill you, so a good shit-kicking will have to do."

John could feel fear running through his body. His pulse raced. He looked around for an escape. The only way was to jump back on the boat. He knew he couldn't get past the man. He would get beaten senseless from his club. The man started walking towards him, slapping the club against the palm of his hand.

"Silly me," said a voice coming down the dock from the clubhouse. "I forgot my car keys on the captain's table. I got to the car before I realized!" It was Suzie.

The man hid the club behind his back and walked past Suzie. He glanced at John. In the dull light, John saw him point his finger at him like a gun and, with his middle finger, mimicked pulling a trigger.

"John, what's the matter?" asked Suzie. "You look like you've seen a ghost."

"I think that man wanted to beat the crap out of me," said John. "He's the son of a patient who had an unfortunate complication. I was the surgeon who helped transport him to another hospital. I think you just saved me!"

"That's crazy!" said Suzie. "You sure you are okay?"

"Let's get your keys," said John.

They hopped on the boat and opened the companionway. After retrieving the keys from the captain's table, they walked to the parking lot together. The man who threatened John was nowhere to be seen. They bid each other good night and headed to their homes.

Chapter 6

"Here's your coffee," said Hans as he handed the cup to John. "What can I help you with?"

Hans Arnold, a senior psychiatrist at the hospital, was 60 years old. He had a slight German accent and was tall and slender. He had thinning grey hair on top of his head and a long, thick grey beard. His gentle eyes were blue and fixated on John as he seemed to gather information by observing John's body language. John had a pain in his upper abdomen and a tightness in his chest that occurred when he was anxious. He could feel his eyes darting around the room, finally landing on Hans. John was trying to find a comfortable position for his hands, another annoying tic resulting from his free-floating anxiety.

John was visiting Hans reluctantly. Yesterday, he was performing a laparoscopic anterior resection of the rectum for carcinoma with the general surgery resident. The surgery was going well, with John helping the resident. The resident was dissecting the right lateral pelvic sidewall when suddenly there was massive bleeding. John continued to stare at the bleeding as if in a trance while it filled the pelvis with blood.

The anesthesiologist cried out, "I can't keep the blood pressure. I think he is going to arrest!" John stared at the monitor as the blood continued to pour out.

"Dr. Hegland," said the resident calmly, "I think we should do a laparotomy!"

"Yes, yes, of course," said John, as he snapped out of his trance. John reached for the scalpel and created a large incision. The resident, using the sucker, evacuated the blood while John placed sponges in the pelvis to put pressure on the bleeding iliac vein. The anesthesiologist transfused 2 units of blood while John and the resident placed sutures to close the hole in the iliac vein. When the patient was hemodynamically stable, they completed the rest of the surgery uneventfully. They transferred the patient to the recovery room in a stable condition.

In the recovery room, the resident said, "Dr. Hegland, are you OK? You seemed to freeze when we had that bleeding. Sorry I created it. It's my fault. I'm so sorry."

John looked at the resident and said, "It's not your fault. You did the best that you could. I think that the patient should do fine now. You did a good job helping me. Let's talk with the family."

John was admonishing himself for not reacting quickly enough to the bleeding emergency. Part of the training as a surgeon was to react to bleeding and other unexpected events during surgery and repair the damage appropriately. John knew he had failed to do that. He was lucky the resident was with him to help get the problem fixed. John thought he knew why he was slow to react.

"Thanks for agreeing to see me," John said to Hans. "I am having difficulties concentrating." John relayed the events of yesterday's surgery. "I worry about making another mistake at surgery, causing a patient to suffer. A few months ago, a gynecologist put a trocar through the aorta. His wife had run off with their Roman Catholic parish priest. In my role as chief, I met with the gynecologist. He was an excellent surgeon, and his accidental surgical error was out of character. I suggested that his marital difficulties contributed to the surgical mistake. He broke down in my office and started crying. I asked him to get professional help."

Hans stroked his long beard while he looked at John thoughtfully. "Are you having difficulties in your marriage?"

John had been married to Marie for 12 years. They had 2 children, Ainslie, age 12, and Claudia, age 10. They had experienced the usual difficulties that had been in marriage, but lately, the problems seemed insurmountable. The latest difficulties resulted in the frequent trips Marie was taking to Florida. They were arguing the night before the surgery, and it resulted in them sleeping in separate rooms. John slept badly that night and woke up unrested.

"You spend your days at the hospital," Marie said. "Everyone admires you. My girlfriends tell me I am lucky to have you as my husband. You get your ego boosted everywhere you go. Nobody says you are lucky to have me as a wife. I am bored out of my mind looking after 2 kids while you get all the admiration. The perfect husband with the perfect family."

"I can understand you wanting to get away, but this is the 4th time in 6 weeks you have flown off to Florida," said John. "It's like you don't want to be with us."

"I don't feel useful around here," said Marie. A tear rolled down her cheek. "You do all the shopping and drive the kids to their activities. When the house is a mess, you clean it up. It's like you go through life like there are no problems. No one needs me here. In Florida, I feel free. Just breathing the salt air makes me feel alive. I met a group of German students. One fellow named Karl was having difficulties. Karl's parents were in an automobile accident in Germany. Although they are recovering in hospital, it devastated Karl. I need to help him. That is why I am going back so often."

"I need you here," said John softly.

"Fuck you!" retorted Marie. "You only need your weak ego boosted by parading around the hospital as chief of surgery. I'm bringing Karl back with me this time to show him around Toronto. Maybe we'll drive to Quebec. He has a week off school."

John's jaw dropped. Conflicting thoughts flashed through his mind. This was craziness. How can things spin out of control so quickly? What was the matter with Marie? This was a good life they had built. They had a house, 2 beautiful children, and a life that others could only dream about. None of this made sense. Maybe there was something wrong with Marie.

Anger blazed through John. "He is not to set foot in this house! If you head down this path of self-destruction, you are on your own. I think you need professional help!" yelled John.

Marie's eyes narrowed, and she kicked her foot into John's groin. John let out a groan as he clutched his crotch and fell to the floor. "Fuck you!" she cried out and then stormed out of the room and into the spare bedroom. John heard the door lock. John lay there for a moment in disbelief. This couldn't be happening, thought John.

John relayed this recent development in his marriage to Hans. "I think there is something wrong with her," said John. "I need to strategize so I can concentrate. I don't want the same thing to happen again while I'm doing surgery."

Hans continued to stroke his beard. "The first thing you need to realize is that there are always two sides to a story. It's very common for one partner to feel ignored while perceiving the other to be in a higher societal position. Often, the female is the one to put her career on hold while we men advance ours. The resentment from the imbalance results in marital conflicts. Would you be amenable to marital counseling? Do you think she would be agreeable to marital counseling?"

"I'm keen to do anything to fix this, but when I have broached the subject with her, she refuses," said John.

Changing the subject, Hans asked, "What do you think happened at the operation that prevented you from dealing with the bleeding?"

"Well, I was tired from not sleeping well," responded John. "I had anxiety with a pain in my stomach before the operation. I felt nauseous and restless. Once the operation started, this settled until the bleeding started. I felt like I was dreaming. I wanted to do something, but I couldn't move. It was almost as if, when the resident asked me if I wanted to do a laparotomy, it granted permission for me to leap into action."

"Have you considered strategies in the future?" asked Hans.

"Yes," said John. "If I ever felt like that again before starting an operation, I would see if another surgeon could do the case. If there were no one, I would cancel the case until I felt better."

Hans said, "I think a meeting with me once a week for the next few months may also help you. Talking about these complex relationship problems will help you work through them. Unlike surgery, where you can remove a tumor, the patient will get better. Often, there is no simple solution, and you will need to face the decision of acceptance or the alternative. So, you must be prepared for the alternative, which often involves separation or divorce. I'm going to give a name for a divorce lawyer. You can decide whether you want to see her, but I think it is important for you to know what the law expects from each of you, even if you can solve this complex problem. You need to know about the alternative."

John went quiet. Divorce was not something he had ever considered. He could feel his anxiety returning. His hands were looking for a comfortable position. There was a tightness in his chest, and he felt he was having trouble breathing. "I don't think I could manage a divorce right now. The thought terrifies me," said John.

"What are you worried about?" asked Hans.

John thought about that briefly before responding, "I worry about the kids and how it will affect them. I worry about being alone. She will financially ruin me. Of that, I am certain."

Hans calmly replied. "To address your first concern about the kids. They are resilient. If you think they don't know what is happening, you fool yourself. The children will pick up non-verbal clues from your anxiety and misinterpret them. They might think they are the ones causing you to be upset. They will appreciate your honesty and trust you if you discuss this with them when the time is right.

"Your second concern is about being alone. Well, you are alone now and have been for some time. A divorce will not add to your loneliness.

"Addressing your last concern, finances. To stay with someone because of money, well, that is despicable."

A stony silence filled the room while John considered what Hans had said, especially the last point. John's anxiety disappeared. Hans was right. In a matter of seconds, Hans had dissolved his concerns. Why he couldn't come up with that on his own explains why professional help is so important. John sighed in relief. "Thanks, Hans. I feel a weight lifted off my shoulders."

"So next week, then?" inquired Hans.

"Absolutely," said John with renewed confidence.

Chapter 7

The ringing cell phone woke him. It was 2 AM. Getting woken up in the middle of the night for a surgeon was common. Getting woken up on a night when he was not on call for the emergency room was unusual. John answered the phone.

A voice said, "Sorry to wake you. I'm calling from the coroner's office. One of your surgeons, Joe Sawchuk, drove his car into the lake and died. We found your business card in his wallet. We are going to do an autopsy in the morning. I thought you should know. We are trying to track down his next of kin. Do you know who that might be?"

John was at a loss for words. This was a real shock. After all the trauma Joe had been through battling alcoholism, and now this. John finally said, "I don't know who you could contact. Joe had alcohol problems a few years back. His wife left him. Not sure if she is still in Canada. I recall Joe saying she moved back to the UK to live with her sister in Yorkshire. I know his adult children haven't spoken to him for years. He used to joke about that. I think they are still living in Ontario. Sorry, I couldn't have been more helpful."

"Thanks for this information. I'm sure we will track them down," said the voice. John hung up the phone after thanking the person on the other line for calling.

John lay in bed now, totally awake. His wife, Marie, was in Florida, so he was in bed alone. John was in shock at the news. There would be much to sort out at the hospital in the morning. Although he thought he could not go back to sleep, he drifted off into a restless slumber. The alarm went off at 5:30 and woke him up. He had been through a lot over the past 48 hours, so he welcomed whatever rest he could get.

John arrived at the hospital and went to the chief of staff's office. Nigel was exercising on his Peloton while answering his emails on the computer fixed to the front of the stationary bicycle. John knocked on his door and opened it.

"Nigel, can I have a word?" asked John.

Nigel pushed the stop button and hopped off the peloton. "Come in and have a seat. What can I help you with?" asked Nigel.

"I got a call from the coroner's office last night," said John. "They found Joe Sawchuk dead in his car after the car drove into the lake."

Nigel went quiet as he watched John. After a few seconds, John spoke. "They are going to do an autopsy today. I thought I would drop by the coroner's office. They are trying to find the next of kin. I hoped to review his medical affairs file to see if anyone was listed."

Nigel asked, "Do you think he was drinking again? Didn't he have an alcohol problem a few years back? This was before I started working here."

"I spoke with his addiction specialist, Graham, a few days ago," said John. "He says there is no way he was drinking again. He was quite emphatic. Graham told me that Joe was the poster child for alcohol reform. The urine tests were all negative, and he attends the meetings religiously. Joe was quite open to discussing his success. He brought it up during the discussion about the complication from cholecystectomy at the morbidity and mortality meeting."

"Once an alcoholic, always an alcoholic," said Nigel. "I suspect the stress of his latest surgical disaster tipped him over the edge."

John shook his head, then looked at Nigel and said, "You have no basis to say that! I worked with him closely, and Graham's assessment was accurate. I know this guy. There was no way he would kill himself after everything he had been through. The only thought that comes to my mind is your discomfort with dealing with him. It is no longer your problem to deal with him now that he is dead. You are happy now. You don't have to explain the terrible impression it gives the press about how the hospital manages a surgeon's complication."

"John, you are a pain in the ass," shouted Nigel. "Get the fuck out of here!"

John stood up and glared at Nigel. His respect for Nigel's leadership plummeted even deeper than after the medical advisory meeting. This was no time to speak badly about someone who had just died. Joe had been on staff at the hospital for over 25 years. Certainly, he had difficulties during this time, but anyone in Nigel's position should know that life is tough. How someone as callous as Nigel could get into such a position of power reflected a failure in the medical administrative selection system. John turned around and left.

John operated during the day. On his list were 4 laparoscopic inguinal hernia repairs and 2 laparoscopic cholecystectomies. The resident assigned to John was Sarah. She was in her last year of training. After 5 years of surgical training, she had perfected her techniques, so the operations went flawlessly. The day went quickly, and John finished early, at 2:30 in the afternoon. John glanced at his watch. He had time to walk to the coroner's office before his 4 PM Department of Surgery meeting. The next of kin listed in Joe's medical file was his oldest son, Bruce. There was a phone number saved in the medical file. He had called the coroner's office with the number earlier in the morning. They told him that by 2 PM, they should have finished the autopsy.

The coroner's office was a block away from the hospital. John entered the building and went through security. He uneventfully walked through the sensors and metal detectors and up to the second floor. Several years ago, someone stormed through the doors with a gun. Fortunately, he had not loaded it. The perpetrator gave up the gun after a police negotiator convinced him it was best. No one was hurt, but they installed metal detectors, offering the staff an extra layer of safety.

A receptionist named Tammy was on a sign at the front of the desk. "Hi Tammy," said John to the receptionist. "I was speaking with Derek Tan, the pathologist, earlier. He said I could drop around to discuss a case."

"Sure," said Tammy. "He's expecting you. Have a seat while I call him."

John sat down. A television monitor with a 24-hour news station was in the waiting room. Nigel's face appeared. The reporter was asking him a question. The camera focused on Nigel. "Unfortunately, Dr. Sawchuk died from an automobile accident last night. On behalf of the hospital, I extend my condolences to the family. Joe Sawchuk was a valued member of the medical staff."

"I understand they found an empty bottle of scotch on the passenger seat," stated the reporter. "Didn't Dr. Sawchuk have an alcohol problem?"

"This was a surprise for us as well because he had a successful treatment," said Nigel. "Alcoholism is a terrible disease. The pressures of a surgical practice likely caused him to have a relapse."

John's jaw dropped. To give that kind of information when likely the family did not know the details was inappropriate. The autopsy results take weeks before all the testing, including toxicology, comes back. John couldn't shake the feeling there was more to the story. He felt Nigel was using Joe's death to get his name plastered over the media. John could not come up with any other reason for Nigel to have his face and name over the news channel, other than he wanted the publicity. John was still staring at the screen when Derek Tan tapped him on the shoulder, causing him to jump.

"Sorry," said Derek. "I didn't mean to startle you."

"Derek, good to see you," said John. "I was watching the news. Nigel Gilman, our chief of staff at the hospital, claims Joe died in a drunken stupor. How could he get that information so quickly?"

"Let's go into my office," said Derek. "This building leaks information like a sieve. My office is private."

John and Derek went through a door that required a pass key and down a short hall to Derek's office. Derek sat behind a large wooden desk, and John sat in the seat facing the desk. Derek was in his early 30s and of Oriental background. He was slender and had short black hair with bangs covering his forehead. Derek wore thick horn-rimmed glasses but would remove them to see things when they were close. His family emigrated to Canada before he was born.

John and Derek had gone to medical school together. They were friends and sat in the back of the classes together during the first 2 years of medical school. They drifted apart when John underwent his surgery training and Derek underwent a pathology residency. Years later, they reconnected when they realized they were working within a block of each other. John felt lucky to have a contact in the coroner's office. Derek could alert him when the chief coroner was leveling concerns about a death in his surgical department.

"There was a police report leaked to the press," said Derek. "It detailed the accident and the shocker about the empty bottle of scotch on the passenger seat."

"Wow," said John, shaking his head. "That is a surprise to me. I spoke with his addiction specialist, who said there was no way he could be drinking."

"Don't be jumping to conclusions just yet," said Derek. "There is more to this story than an empty bottle. I'm not sure how much I should tell you. I suspect you will tell your chief of staff and the CEO, but please don't tell the press until all the results are back."

John looked at Derek quizzically. "Of course. I'll keep it quiet. The press has already labeled me as a villain. I have no plans to talk with anyone from the press."

"Although there was an empty bottle in the car, the stomach was empty," explained Derek. "I did an alcohol 'spot' check on his urine, and it was negative. I will have to wait for the toxicology results to confirm there was no alcohol or drugs in his urine. I sent the blood off for toxicology, but if the urine is negative, so will the blood. This means that alcohol had nothing to do with the death.

"Another thing. His lungs remained free of water despite submerging the car in the lake. Sure, it can happen with drowning when the vocal cords go into laryngospasm, but when someone is drunk, they suck water into their lungs."

"The other anomaly is that someone fractured his larynx. This caused his death. We see this with strangulation. A fractured larynx causes asphyxiation, making it impossible for the lungs to fill with air. Joe was dead before the car went into the lake. Also, petechiae ruptured blood vessels in the whites of his eyes. This only happens when someone strangles a person."

The Complication

John was quiet. He felt his eyes bulge as the information sunk in. John said, "You mean someone killed Joe? That's wild! Why would someone do that...." He stopped speaking in mid-sentence. John looked directly at Derek. John recounted the story behind Joe's cholecystectomy complication and the angry family. He described his two encounters with the son. He suggested the family may have had something to do with it.

"Look," said Derek. "As a pathologist, I report the facts and let the police sort out the rest. You should go to the police station and speak with the officer in charge of the case, Sidney Noseworthy. If the family is going to this trouble, your life might be in danger. Let me give Sidney a call now."

Derek used the speakerphone and connected with Sidney. Derek reviewed the pathological findings. He described the fractured larynx from strangulation as the cause of death. John relayed his interaction with the angry family. John agreed to come to the precinct to give a statement later in the evening after the Department of Surgery meeting.

The familiar tightness in John's chest and difficulty breathing because of anxiety resurfaced as he drove home from the precinct. His wife was still in Florida, and he hadn't heard from her. His two children were at home alone. He worried that someone might come after him to his home. Perhaps his kids should stay with his parents for a few weeks. He knew the kids would never agree to that.

His cell phone rang. The screen lit up with the name. It was his friend Paul, the hepatobiliary surgeon. John pressed the answer button on the steering wheel. Paul said, "Brian Feldman just died. I thought you should know."

Chapter 8

Miriam was at the bedside when her father passed away. The doctors had predicted he would stop breathing within a few hours. After taking him off the ventilator, he didn't take his last breath until 6 hours later. It had been a rough time for her and her brothers. After the second operation, they transferred him to the intensive care unit. He had many post-operative complications.

The medical team transfused him as he continued to bleed. His kidneys failed, and they started him on hemodialysis. He was septic and given antibiotics, but they could not get the blood pressure above 80 systolic, even with high-dose vasopressors. He remained unconscious on the ventilator. On the second post-op day had a massive hemorrhagic stroke, leaving him paralyzed on his right side.

"There's not much more we can do," said Dr. Speakman, the ICU doctor. The two brothers and Mariam were sitting in the ICU waiting room. "He's on the maximum treatment. The stroke had caused permanent brain damage. My advice is to withdraw the ventilator support. I will give you a few minutes to discuss among yourselves."

Rick stood up and approached Dr. Speakman. His face was red, and his eyes narrowed. "You keep him alive! We'll let you know when to let him go! If anything happens to him, you will regret it." Rick was hyperventilating, and his muscles were bulging. Fear filled the eyes of Dr. Speakman.

"Look," said Dr. Speakman calmly, "we will do nothing without talking with you first. I think you must understand 'though, he will probably not survive another 24 hours. There's nothing we can do about that." He was used to speaking with troubled families, but this man frightened him.

Dr. Speakman answered a few of their questions, then went back to his rounds. Miriam had been dealing with the brother's anger all her life. Their reluctance to withdraw treatment was not based on moral grounds. Miriam knew it was not because they liked their father. In fact, they hated him. The reason they were so upset was that their father was involved with cryptocurrency and had the money stashed somewhere on the internet. He frequently told them to be nice, or they wouldn't see a cent. The father also warned them if anything happened to him, the secret stash would remain hidden. He told them many times to make certain he stayed alive.

Brian Feldman was not his real name. He was born in Canada to Italian immigrants. They named him Primo Parente. Primo changed his name after his first big haul of cash. He had flown to Colombia and smuggled into Canada 1 kilogram of cocaine. It was worth $100,000. The smuggling involved placing a gastric balloon into his stomach with a gastroscope. Instead of filling it with a saline solution, he filled it with cocaine. They designed these balloons to stay in the stomach for months originally as a weight loss strategy. There was little chance the balloon would break or deteriorate during transportation.

When he spoke to his bank manager about the cash, he was disappointed to find out that anything over $10,000 had to be reported to the authorities. Primo would be required to prove where he got the money, and he would need to pay income tax on it. The banker's name was Brian Feldman. He spoke with such knowledge and understanding it impressed Primo. He wanted to be like him, so he changed his name. The banker also suggested that he get involved with the new cryptocurrency exchange if he wanted to keep the money hidden.

Before too long, the new Brian Feldman had hired junior college students as mules to transport the cocaine. He paid them $10,000 for a trip that included an uncomfortable procedure involving a balloon insertion and removal in Toronto. Before long, Brian had millions stashed away in cryptocurrency wallets across the internet. Then, he developed gallstone pancreatitis.

The pain was the worst Brian had ever felt. It was in his abdomen and radiated to his back. He called Joe Sawchuk. They knew each other from the substance abuse meetings they both attended weekly. At one point in his life, Brian was hooked on cocaine. His wife had left him, and his kids wouldn't talk to him. He knew he needed to get off the stuff, so he checked himself into a rehabilitation center. Although he kept importing the drug into Canada, he stayed away from using it.

His children did not know how he made his money. They gradually warmed up to him when they figured out he was rich. He did not trust them, especially the boys, because they were violent. More than once, the police had arrested the boys when there was a barroom fight. Usually, the boys would walk away unscathed, but their opponents would not be so lucky. Often, they left their opponents crippled for life. They seemed to get enjoyment out of hurting others.

Joe Sawchuk met him in the emergency room and admitted him to the surgical floor. He organized a CAT scan, IV fluids, and pain medications. When the pain settled a few days later, Joe recommended surgery to remove the gallbladder. His daughter and sons were against performing the surgery. They want him to go to a downtown hospital, not a little community hospital. Brian trusted Joe and wanted to have the surgery with him.

Rick was still seething when Miriam spoke. "There's nothing we can do for him. Even if he lived, there is such extensive brain damage he would never speak again. The most humane thing is to let him go."

"Have you thought about how we are going to retrieve the money locked away in cryptocurrency lockers?" asked Rick. "He's the only one who knows where the money he hid the money."

Miriam was silent for a few seconds. "Now, we may never retrieve the money. There's nothing we can do about that except go through his records after he passes away. Perhaps his accountant or bank manager will know how we can find the stashed money."

Rick shook his head and shouted, "This is bullshit! In this modern day of medicine, surely they can wake him up for just enough time for him to tell us how to do it!" Rick stormed out of the room and down the stairs to the exit. He did not have a steady stream of income. He needed his dad's money, and he was going to get it. To use the skills he possessed, there were only a few who would pay for his services.

He reflected on his last job. He planned to carry this out for free, but then he got the phone call two days ago. "I work for an international organization, and we are looking for someone who can do a job for us," said the voice on the phone.

"What kind of job?" asked Rick.

"Your dad recently had botched surgery," said the voice. "The surgeon needs to go away permanently. I will pay you $10,000 now and $10,000 after you complete the job."

"Who did you say you are?" asked Rick suspiciously.

"I didn't," said the voice. "These are delicate matters, and the less you know, the better. Check your bank account. I'll wait while you do that."

Rick clicked on the bank website. He signed in using his password. He knew he had overdrawn the account by $2000 because he tried to get money out of the ATM earlier in the day, and it denied the request. His eyes widened when he saw the account was in a positive balance of $8000. "Wow!" he said. "How did you do that?"

"We need the job completed by tonight," said the voice. "It must look like an accident. Here's what I want you to do." The voice instructed Rick on how to stage the 'accident'.

Rick drove his car to within a block of Dr. Sawchuk's house. He parked on a side street and walked the rest of the way. The voice on the phone had told him that Dr. Sawchuk was by himself at home. There was a Tesla parked in front of a small house that was plugged into a cord that went under a garage door. Joe looked around to be sure there was no one walking in the street. He rocked the Tesla until the tilt feature triggered the alarm.

The driveway was poorly lit, and Rick hid in the shadows behind a large oak tree that was close to the driver's door. Joe Sawchuk opened the front door of the house and sped down the short pathway to the Tesla. Joe glanced around and saw no one. He pulled out his Tesla keys and pressed the silent feature. He shook his head and said out loud, "Those kids again."

Joe opened the driver's door to see if there was any damage to the interior of his car. At that moment, Rick placed him in a headlock, but in doing so, the momentum threw him off balance. The two of them went crashing into the driver's seat. Rick felt a resounding crunch coming from the front of Joe's neck, and in less than 90 seconds, Joe stopped moving.

Rick put on a pair of latex gloves and moved Joe to the passenger seat. He buckled him in as if he were a passenger. Rick drove to the docks in Toronto Harbor. There was no one at the docks at this time of night. It was easy to move Joe to the driver's side and buckle him in. He emptied the bottle of scotch on Joe's clothing, then closed the door. Joe reached through the window. He put the Tesla in 'drive'. It took a few tries because Rick had to apply the brakes by pushing Joe's knees to engage the vehicle in drive. After getting the correct sequence and then releasing the pressure on Joe's knees, the Tesla rolled into the lake. The rear of the Tesla remained out of the water when the front hit the bottom. Joe walked back to the main road and took the transit trolley to his local downtown bar. He made sure he paid for his first drink with his credit card and watched the rest of the baseball game with the bartender. He wanted a rock-solid alibi. The next day, another $10,000 appeared in his account.

Chapter 9

"I think someone murdered him," said John. "I spoke with the coroner's office yesterday afternoon. Joe had a fractured larynx. They are concluding the cause of death was strangulation." John was sitting in Nigel's office. It was 7 AM, the morning after he visited with the coroner. John hesitated to meet with Nigel because of their history, but felt it was necessary to update him. John was spending the day doing outpatient endoscopies and needed to be at the clinic before 8 o'clock, so it was important to meet with him early.

"What are you talking about?" cried Nigel. "You've got no right to talk to the coroner. This is a hospital business. You need to stay in your lane."

"I also spoke to the police," said John, ignoring Nigel's last comment. "I think I know who killed him. The son has threatened me on two occasions."

"You are paranoid," stated Nigel. "Before you jump to conclusions, you need to think things through. You have no right to go to the police and drag the hospital through the mud. Your actions put us in an awkward position. Have you thought about that?"

John stared at Nigel incredulously. "What is the matter with you? One of our surgeons got murdered. I got threatened. Are you concerned only about the reputation of the hospital? Have you thought about what you are saying?" John got up and stormed out of Nigel's office. As John walked to his car, he vowed to avoid another meeting with the self-absorbed chief of staff whenever possible. The aggravation he caused him made the visits painful.

Nigel was seething at his office. He was on his Peloton, pedaling as fast as he could push himself. He could use a robust anaerobic session to exorcise the frustration he felt coursing through his body. Rebecca said she would take care of things but needed his $20,000. What the hell had she done? He wanted the bad press to go away. Joe killing himself would have caused the press to have sympathy for the hospital. If it was true someone murdered him, an entirely new level of investigation was going to happen. There would be questions about staff safety and what he was going to do as chief of staff. He needed to speak with Rebecca. Nigel called her. The call went directly to voicemail. "Call me as soon as you get this," he said to the voicemail.

Nigel walked down the hallway to the CEO's office. He thought he better update her on the possibility that someone murdered Joe and what that might mean for the hospital. When he reached her door, he had second thoughts. Before discussing the possibility of murder, maybe there was a way of turning this around. He needed to talk to Rebecca.

Rebecca called him an hour later. Nigel told her about the coroner's suspicions of strangulation as a cause of death. "I thought you said my problem would disappear," said Nigel.

"I think I told you that you don't want to know how it would go away, and I suggest you remember that." Rebecca reminded Nigel. "None of this is going to come back on you. I don't want to discuss this with you over the phone or anywhere else. Just leave it, Nigel. I know what I am doing. I'll see you tonight." With that, she hung up the phone.

Nigel did a Google search for doctors who unhappy patients had murdered. There was an article about 15 doctors murdered in Italy by unhappy patients or their families. In China, there were 22 case reports, but the article explained there was a poor collection of cases because of censorship. Someone anonymously submitted a letter to the editor of an obscure Western journal. Authorities suppressed the news of over 500 recorded cases, as it might make China feel unsafe. Chinese doctors getting beaten up was a regular occurrence in the news. Workplace violence against doctors was a major deterrent in China for recruits in the medical profession.

A social media post was from a woman who recently immigrated to Canada from China. She claimed that someone murdered her husband. He was a surgeon in the north of China, and a patient died following a plastic surgery procedure. The cause of death of the surgeon was a severe beating resulting in brain hemorrhage. No one ever caught the assailant. The wife was herself a physician and feared for her life as well. This was the basis for granting her asylum in Canada. She was grateful for the opportunity for a new life in Canada. Although she felt safe in Canada, she mentioned she kept her identity on social media postings a secret. Her parents were still living in China, and she was worried something might happen to them.

The wife of the deceased surgeon explained she was friends with a cousin of the patient who died. They went to high school together and would meet for a drink after work every 2 weeks. It was this cousin who advised her to leave China. The cousin told her the family had paid the equivalent of $50,000 to have her husband killed. Her death was to be part of the package as well. The threat of getting murdered brought her to Canada.

Nigel sat back in his chair and thought about what he had read. Doctors are getting killed by angry patients and families in many countries. The motivation seems to be revenge after a bad outcome. 'An eye for an eye' type thing. That this would occur in Canada seemed so unlikely. The best revenge is to sue the doctor and, if successful, walk away with a huge cash settlement. Litigation against doctors was a long, drawn-out process with a high failure rate. It took an average of 6 years to be successful, but the failure rate for the patient was 93%. Only 7% of litigation goes in favor of the plaintiff. Perhaps that might be what drives a patient or family to have their doctor killed in a country like Canada.

Nigel thought about what John Hegland had told him. John said that the son Rick picked him up and smashed his head against the drywall when he talked with him about the complication. A few days later, Rick approaches John at the yacht club and threatens to beat him up. John said he mentioned something about getting paid to do that. "What had Rebecca done?" Nigel asked in his empty office. If what he was thinking was correct, that Rebecca orchestrated this, it could destroy his life as he knew it.

Nigel put on his coat and headed out of the office. He needed to control the damage and deflect any attention away from himself. He would make certain that John Hegland took the fall for this.

Chapter 10

John arrived home after he met with Sidney Noseworthy, the investigator assigned to Joe Sawchuk's case. Sidney's lack of conviction about this being a murder was clear to John. Sidney explained it was too early in the investigation to conclude the death resulted from murder. "I can understand a family getting upset about a complication after surgery, but resorting to murder, I have never heard of that," said Sidney.

"Regarding Rick, we have arrested him for disorderly conduct and aggressive behavior. Most of the time, it involved bar fights, and although he had badly beaten up the other guys, they refused to lay charges, so we let him go. Without a doubt, he is violent, so you need to take extra precautions."

Sidney brushed him off and said, "I'll keep you updated."

As John was driving home, he couldn't help but wonder what was wrong with Nigel and Sidney. Maybe he was making too much of the situation and letting his imagination get the best of him. The autopsy findings were clear. Someone had crushed Joe's larynx and had gone to a lot of trouble to make it look like an alcohol-related death.

"Are you and Mom getting divorced?" asked Ainslie when John arrived home that night. Ainslie was sitting in front of her computer. She turned her swivel chair to face her father when he entered her room. Despite the door being open, John softly knocked on it.

"Why would you ask that?" responded John.

"I heard you arguing before she left for Florida," said Ainslie. "She seems to be in a bad mood most of the time with us. I cleaned my room, and she didn't even notice."

"Mom's going through a difficult time right now. We must be understanding," explained John. "She loves you and Claudia. You need to remember that."

A tear rolled down Ainslie's cheek. Her eyes became wet. She wiped away the tears with the sleeve of her sweater. In less than a second, she was sobbing.

"Honey, everything will be okay," said John, reaching down to hug Ainslie. Ainslie hugged her dad tightly as she cried onto his shoulder. "Don't worry about mom. Focus on yourself. At 12 years old, things will make much more sense to you as you age. You have a lot of wisdom and insight for a 12-year-old."

Ainslie stopped crying. "It's not the mom I am worried about. It's you." She let go of her dad and swiveled in her chair. She turned to her computer and pecked on the keyboard.

"What are you worried about?" asked John.

Ainslie didn't answer and kept banging on the keyboard. John let the conversation hang in silence as Ainslie concentrated on the computer. After a minute, Ainslie stopped working the keyboard and said, "Look at this."

John looked at the computer screen but didn't understand what he saw. He shook his head, confused, as his eyes scanned the computer screen. There were a series of numbers and computer codes on the screen. His name, John Hegland, appeared in the middle of the screen. Another series of codes and numbers followed the name. "What does this mean?" he asked.

"Dad, someone has it out for you," said Ainslie. "Someone wants to hurt you. I came across this by accident. I wanted to find out if there was anything about you and mom on the internet. You may have heard about the dark web. It is not all bad, and I do nothing illegal about logging on to it. In many countries where they censor online content, it is the only way to communicate. I think this came from China. Dad, what have you done to get someone so angry with you?"

"How can you tell from what is on the screen?" asked John.

"Dad!" sighed Ainslie, exasperated. "It's so obvious. I'm not going to give you a lesson on the internet. What's the matter with you? You must be more careful about who you share your personal information with."

John smiled. His 12-year-old was lecturing him on internet safety. He was dating himself. He recognized he was internet illiterate, but having his daughter point out his weaknesses was something he never expected. Ainslie clicked on some lines of numbers and code. A website appeared in Chinese characters. Ainslie clicked on something else, and the English translation appeared. It was a website offering investment advice. An oriental woman was holding a piece of paper, smiling.

"I need a password to get into the site," said Ainslie.

"It seems like someone lost something during the translation," said John. "This doesn't seem harmful." After looking at what Ainslie pulled up on the computer, John was not concerned. How she concluded someone wanted to hurt him was not obvious to him.

Ainslie shook her head and looked at her dad incredulously. "Dad, just be careful. Something is happening, and I don't know what it is."

John changed the subject. "Ainslie, I have a sailboat booked in the 2nd week of December in Antigua for 10 days. Your mom is not going now. Do you and Claudia want to come with me? I have a few others from my racing crew that are coming."

"Dad, I am 12 years old!" retorted Ainslie. "There is no way I will spend 10 days locked up on a boat with you and your boring friends." She turned to her computer, and John saw she was working on a history assignment. "I have to finish this assignment tonight," she said.

He was leaving for a sailing vacation in 2 weeks. Initially, when he organized the trip 6 months ago, he planned to go with Marie. There were 3 cabins on the sailboat, so he invited 2 other couples to come along as well. One couple had canceled last week. John's parents were planning to stay with Ainslie and Claudia. The last time John broached the subject of the trip a few weeks ago to Marie, her comments were like Ainslie's. She said it would be boring and didn't want to go. John had scheduled time off work, and the $8000 deposit was nonrefundable.

John smiled again. Ainslie was growing up to be a woman of strong opinions. After telling her not to stay up too late, he kissed her on the top of her head and left her room. His cell phone went off. It was Derek Tan, the pathologist. John answered.

"I think someone just tried to kill me," said Derek.

Chapter 11

Nigel was pacing the floor of his penthouse apartment in downtown Toronto. There was a spectacular view of Toronto Harbor on one side. Through the other floor-to-ceiling window, a view of the CN Tower lit up with LED lights that changed colors every few seconds. Nigel's face was red, and his bulging eyes revealed the anger coursing through his body.

"Rebecca, what the hell is going on?" shouted Nigel. "John Hegland comes marching into my office this morning claiming that someone murdered Joe Sawchuk. I gave you $20,000 expecting a top-notch publicity campaign describing my excellent leadership skills to groom me for the top job as Deputy Minister of Health. Now, they will link me to a negative event, the murder of a surgeon. What did you use the money for?"

"Calm down," said Rebecca. "Everything is under control."

"Under control, my ass," yelled Nigel. "Explain how my $20,000 investment will make my problems disappear!"

Rebecca looked up at Nigel. "There are a few things you should know. The coroner's report is going to say that Joe Sawchuk's death was an accidental death from alcohol intoxication. The pathologist was stepping out of his area of expertise by concluding someone had strangled him. I have spoken to the chief coroner, who is taking over the case. I need this to go away as well. We can have a press conference in 2 days. As chief of staff, you can discuss physician wellness and all the great things you have done to improve the work environment of the doctors. You can discuss all the programs available for them. We'll organize a wellness expert to chime in as well. You will recognize you can't save everyone, but you are holding his chief, John Hegland, responsible for not giving him the help he needed. We can rehearse beforehand, so you'll come across as a star."

Nigel calmed down after these words reassured him. He felt his pulse slow and the flushed sensation in his face settle as Rebecca talked. After a few minutes, the thought of his money crossed his mind, "Where did the $20,000 end up then?" asked Nigel.

Rebecca went quiet again. "Look, all you need to know is what I told you. As a problem, Joe Sawchuk will melt away, and we will turn the fiasco around. The result will be a public relations event to promote you. The current Deputy Minister of Health has not yet vacated the position, but everyone knows it is a matter of time before he resigns. We will make you look like the perfect person for the position. I know what I am doing."

Nigel relaxed. She was right. She knew what she was doing; he needed to trust her judgment. As assistant to the Deputy Minister of Health, she knew which strings to pull to turn things around.

Nigel knew that John Hegland was the wild card in this and was confident he could control him. There was little risk John would go to the press. Nigel had the power as chief of staff to muzzle any comments from John. He would call him to his office and lay the law down about not going off on the ridiculous tangent that the death was because someone murdered him.

Nigel had met Rebecca at a fundraising function at the hospital. They were sitting at the same table. The affair cost $500 a seat, and Nigel had sponsored an entire table of 10. He left it for Joe Jackson, the public relations officer at the hospital, to find 9 others to sit with him to make it an enjoyable evening for him. Nigel had volunteered to be the MC of the event and promised to give only 2 brief speeches. As was his custom at such events, his speech was all about himself. He made it clear to the audience about his generous gesture of sponsoring a table of ten. In his allotted 10 minutes, he briefed the 1000 people in the room about how great a job he was doing as chief of staff.

Joe Jackson had invited Rebecca as the Ontario Ministry of Health's representative. She arrived late and missed Nigel's speech. When Nigel returned to his seat, he saw Rebecca enter the room and sit beside him. She was wearing a long black dress with a slit that ran up the sides, exposing her beautifully sculpted thighs. She had thick black hair down to her waist. Her face was angelic, without a single wrinkle. Her eyes sparkled. She smiled at him without saying a word, looking softly into his eyes. Nigel couldn't stop staring at her, mesmerized by her beauty. She smelled of fresh flowers, like she had just come out of the shower, causing Nigel to think of what she might look like naked.

Feeling vulnerable by her effect on him, he was also annoyed that she missed what could have been his greatest self-promotion speech ever. Nigel immediately got into an argument with her about healthcare funding. Nigel felt that patients should have to pay for services, and this would reduce the cost of health care. He argued with her to establish his dominance over her. This was something he was very good at; dominating the weaker sex.

"What about the 20% of patients that do not have enough money to pay for food?" argued Rebecca. "How will they pay even a fraction of the health care cost?"

"Look," pointed out Nigel, "why don't we just hand out free food or give everyone free electricity and pay their rent for an apartment? Health care is no different. It's not free. It's expensive. There's no difference between the essential things in life, yet we all must pay for those."

Unable to be intimidated by Nigel's arrogance, Rebecca continued to argue with him. His line of reasoning did not impress her. She ran circles around his weak arguments and by the end of the evening; he agreed with her. The guests said good night as the evening wound down, and the crowd dissipated. Nigel said good night to Rebecca and watched her walk away, mesmerized by the gentle swaying of her hips as she moved. He had never lost an argument like this before, yet he felt he had won. He asked himself, how did she do that? Nigel sat there for a few minutes, thinking about Rebecca. Suddenly, as though he couldn't control himself, he got up from his chair and ran after her. That was how it started 6 months ago.

Chapter 12

"I was walking to the subway station," said Derek. "Out of nowhere, a black car raced up on the curb and tried to run me down from behind. I jumped out of the way just in time." Derek was sitting with John at a bar a block away from Derek's home in north Toronto. They were both drinking draft beer. Derek explained to John over the phone that he was afraid to go home as he lived alone, so John drove to the bar to meet with him.

"Are you sure?" asked John. "Perhaps it was a driver on his cellphone trying to text, and he became distracted. Maybe it was a drunk driver."

Derek was staring at his beer. His hands were still trembling, unable to keep still. His right foot was bouncing up and down in a nervous tic. There was a line of sweat above his eyebrows that was threatening to drip onto the table. It was a full minute before he spoke again. "I can't get the roar from the engine and the sound of the car wheels grinding on the sidewalk out of my head. I feel shaken up."

"Did you call the police?" asked John.

"And tell them what?" asked Derek. "A black car, or perhaps it was dark grey, tried to run me down. It was dark out, and there was no one else around. I doubt they would believe me. Rick physically assaulted you and later verbally threatened you. What have the police done to protect you?"

"Let's go make a report anyway," said John. "I'm sure Sidney Noseworthy will be happy to see me again. It costs nothing, and the event will be on record."

"Another thing," said Derek. "As I was about to leave this evening, Brian Wilson called me into his office. He's the chief coroner. This case has reached the level of the Ontario Ministry of Health. They told him to take over as the pathologist. Brian warned me not to discuss my findings with anyone, especially the press. He would deal with questions coming from them. I think they are going to report he died from alcohol-related problems. John, I'm scared."

"I think we are making too big a deal of this," said John. "Let's finish our beer and head over to the precinct. I'll drive you home afterwards."

The two of them silently guzzled the rest of their beer. They got up from their chairs and headed for the door. The bar had an outdoor parking lot that cost $2 an hour. John had placed the ticket in his windshield when he parked the car. The hour was almost up. "Great timing!" said John. "I feel like I got my money's worth with my $2!"

"You cheap jerk," laughed Derek. "I almost get knocked off and you worry about $2."

A car next to John's had reversed into the adjacent space, but was too close for Derek to open the passenger's door to get in. Derek waited on the pavement so John could back up his car to allow him to get into the passenger seat. John put the car in reverse and slowly backed up. Derek went to open the passenger door. The car blocking John's car suddenly came to life, and Derek froze. His eyes fixated on the rapidly advancing car.

In the fraction of a second it took for Derek to realize the car would hit him, he tried to get into John's car. The car door severed the right leg and the femoral artery at the level of the groin as the passenger door flew off the hinges from the impact. The force pulled Derek away from John's car, throwing him onto the pavement. His head hit the ground with a loud thud before he could let out a scream. The back of the skull went flat from the impact. A stream of blood began flowing from the skull. Blood was pumping from the severed femoral artery onto the pavement in an arch.

John looked directly at Derek immediately before the impact and saw Derek's eyes widen. From the time it took John to turn his head to see the approaching car, the impact had occurred. John screamed, "No, no!" John leaped out of his car as the assailant's car sped away. John immediately went to help his friend. There was a pulsatile stream of blood coming from Derek's right groin. John shoved his hand to apply pressure to the bleeding. The skin at the back of the leg kept the leg still attached, but the impact had shattered the femur. The bony fragments cut John's hand, but he kept the pressure to stop the bleeding. A crowd appeared in a circle around Derek and John. Someone called 911 for an ambulance. Derek was unconscious, and John could see there was also a significant head injury, as brain tissue had oozed out of the open scalp wound.

It took only 2 minutes for the paramedics to arrive. They log-rolled Derek onto the gurney while John maintained pressure in the groin. The attendant started an intravenous and began pumping saline solution into Derek. "I cannot feel a pulse," he said. The calmness in his voice surprised John. The paramedic began cardiac compressions. It took only 13 minutes with lights and sirens to arrive at the trauma center. Shortly after the ambulance attendants took Derek into the trauma room, they pronounced him dead.

John disengaged his hand from Derek's groin. He walked over to the sink in the trauma room and washed the blood off his hands. The trauma room nurse applied a dressing to the laceration just above his 5th finger that the bone fragments had caused. She offered him a tetanus shot, but John just shook his head. He walked over to the waiting police officer.

"We were on our way to visit Sidney Noseworthy at the precinct when another car smashed into us," said John. "I can't believe this has happened." John was shaking his head. The reality of what had occurred sank in, and he could feel his eyes water. He wiped the wetness away with his sleeve. John didn't want anyone to see him crying.

"It's normal to cry after such a tragedy," said the police officer empathetically. "Let me give Sid a call. He may want us to come to the precinct. Are you OK with that?"

John nodded in affirmation. He knew if he tried to talk, he would burst into tears. After finishing the phone call, the police officer ushered John into the police cruiser, and they drove to the precinct. John was in a daze as the officer led him to a small interrogation room with a desk and several chairs. John sat while he waited for Sidney.

A few minutes later, Sidney walked into the room. He was black, with short curly hair cropped close to his scalp. He had a thin mustache and a beard trimmed short. As a homicide detective, he wore a suit with a thin black tie. The muscles of his arms looked like they were about to pop through his tightly fitting suit. He spoke in a deep, commanding voice. "I am so sorry about your friend," he said sympathetically. "The officer from the hospital told me what he knew, but perhaps you could tell me in your own words. Are you okay if we record this?"

John nodded and then recounted the story, beginning again with the visit to the coroner's office. He described the assailant's car as a black Mercedes Benz. After he finished, Sidney asked him some questions, but he could not answer what the driver looked like nor give him the license plate number. After 30 minutes had passed, he was told he could go home, and the same police officer from the hospital drove him there.

The events had drained John of all emotions. When he entered his house, Marie sat in the kitchen with a younger man. They were talking. Marie stopped mid-sentence as John walked into the kitchen and looked up at him with a smile. "John, I'd like you to meet Karl."

John stood momentarily and stared at his wife and then back at the young man. "Look, I'm not myself tonight. I've had a rough time. Can we talk in the morning?" John climbed up the stairs to his bedroom and closed the door. In less than 10 seconds, Marie was in the room. She was shouting at him. The words seemed to bounce off his skin as he watched her face go red and the veins in her forehead bulge. He was having difficulty putting what she was saying into context. He understood the last thing she said as she bolted out of the room. "I want a divorce!" she screamed.

Chapter 13

When John woke up, it was still dark outside. It was 6 AM. The house was quiet as he entered the kitchen. He knew Claudia and Ainslie were still sleeping. John would get them up at 7 AM for them to catch their 7:30 AM school bus. He didn't know if Marie and her new friend stayed overnight. John pressed the button on the espresso machine, and in less than a minute, there was a demitasse of hot espresso. He knocked it back and then made another one. As the machine was grinding the coffee for his next cup, he turned around and noticed a brown manila envelope on the kitchen island. Written in large letters in a black felt pen was his name. John opened the envelope and pulled out the contents. It was a file labeled 'Separation Agreement.' John sighed and placed the thick stack of papers back into the envelope. He couldn't face reading what it said this morning. Maybe he would review it tonight, or possibly tomorrow. There was too much on his mind with the events of the accident for him to concentrate.

On the drive to the hospital, John reviewed in his head what he would tell his CEO of the hospital when he met with her at 8 AM. John had called her on the cell phone at 6:30, knowing she would already be at her desk, to ask her if they could meet. She agreed. Nancy had been with the hospital for the last 20 years and worked her way up to the CEO position 3 years ago. She was in her early

60s. She wore large glasses in front of her blue eyes. They would absorb the body language clues about the person she was about to meet, but her eyes would reveal nothing about herself. She prided herself on the ability to know what problem you were going to present to her before you sat in front of her on one of her cushioned chairs. A solution to the problem would be formulated in her mind even before you opened your mouth to speak. This morning, though, John caught her off guard, and for the first time, it was as though she was at a loss for words.

He was sitting in front of her desk, describing the events of the previous night. "I've known Derek for almost 15 years. I have never seen him so scared. Although the police are calling it a hit and run, likely from a drunk driver, Derek told me someone tried to run him down earlier in the evening. We were on our way to report it to the police when the Mercedes Benz attacked us."

Nancy stared at John. Her eyes widened as he recounted what Derek had told him about the autopsy. The coroner's office would likely change his report to an alcohol-related death rather than a death from strangulation. "There is no way Joe Sawchuk was drinking again. I spoke with Dr. Graham, his addiction doctor, who confirmed the urine tests were all negative. He described Joe as the poster child for addiction rehabilitation. I have never smelled alcohol on his breath since he came out of rehab."

Nancy shifted uncomfortably in her chair as John discussed Nigel's response to Derek's pathology findings. "I don't trust Nigel," said John. "I think he will take whatever position that will put him in the most favorable light."

John was about to say something else when her intercom buzzed from her assistant. Nancy picked up the phone and, after a few seconds, said, "okay, thanks. I'll turn on the TV now." She turned to John and said, "Nigel's giving a press conference on Channel 7."

Nancy flipped on the TV, and Nigel's face appeared on the big screen on the wall in front of her desk. "The pathology report has come back, confirming what I told you a few days ago. This is an alcohol-related accident, causing death. There is an enormous amount of stress among our medical staff, who must deal with life-and-death situations daily. Joe was especially vulnerable. It is the role of the chief of the department to identify those at risk and offer them help. Our current chief of surgery failed to do that. I am launching an investigation into why the chief failed one of our most respected surgeons in the community. It is sad to see when a tragedy could have easily been avoided by identifying those at risk and offering them help. I have made my career in teaching leadership. Teaching leadership is only possible for those who are willing to learn. We cannot teach some physicians leadership. Arrogance and self-interest will often get in the way. I will get to the bottom of this. Thank you."

The camera flipped back to Ashley. "There you have it. A committed chief of staff willing to do what it takes to make a less stressful environment for our hard-working doctors." Nancy turned the TV off.

Both Nancy and John continued to stare at the blank screen. Finally, Nancy spoke. "Well, he certainly threw you under the bus, didn't he?"

"Now you know why I cannot work with him," said John. "I do not understand why he is doing all this. There must be a reason he wants me out of the picture. To do this on the news is sinking to the bottom level. I would never expect this from a chief of staff."

"Look," said Nancy, "if it is any consolation for you, I believe what you have told me. You have no reason to make something like this up. I do not have a lot of control over Nigel. We both report to the board of directors separately. I could lodge a formal complaint with the board and ask for a hearing, but it would fail. All the board members see him as a God-like figure who is the savior of our hospital. They fully accept his arrogant statements as strong leadership. They have mentioned frequently this is exactly what the hospital needs to attain the status of 'the best community hospital' in Canada."

John looked at Nancy and smiled before he spoke. "Thank you," he whispered. "It's not just me then. I'm not sure what I am going to do. I'll try to keep a low profile." Just then, his cellphone vibrated. He retrieved it from his pocket and glanced at the number.

He looked up at Nancy with concern written on his face. Nancy said, "it's Nigel, isn't it? Don't answer it. He'll want to meet with you and ask you to step down as chief. Avoid him as long as possible."

John stared at Nancy incredulously. He thought to himself, how does she do that?

Chapter 14

Rebecca smiled as she watched her lover ingratiate himself with the listening television audience. He was very bold and clever at manipulating the press. A few days ago, he had admonished Ashley, the news reporter, for sandbagging him during an interview without preparing him ahead of time. Now Ashley was gushing kind words and admiration for his exceptional leadership skills. Everything was coming into place. She could not allow the report of Joe Sawchuk's death to come out as a murder. The only other two people who knew the truth were Rick, who probably would have done the deed for free, and John Hegland, whom Nigel had publicly emasculated. If John tried to say anything different from Nigel, they would realize he was trying to save his own skin as chief.

Rebecca thought back to 15 years ago. She was visiting her grandparents in a small town in northern China, Qiqihar. Her grandfather was in surgery for a bowel obstruction while she waited in a surgical waiting room with 15 members of their family. When the surgeon came to speak with them, they all stood up and surrounded him. He explained that the cancer had spread to the liver. He managed the bowel obstruction by giving him a colostomy, a bag taped to the side of his abdomen where the stool collects. The family had a lot of questions. He spent the next 30 minutes answering them.

The oldest son, Rebecca's uncle Quan, asked, "When are you going to remove the cancer?"

"It's not possible," said the surgeon. "The cancer is too advanced. If we attempted to remove it, he likely would not survive because it involves important structures. If he survived the surgery, the cancer would undoubtedly recur."

The waiting room became silent. Quan became red in the face, and his eyes were bulging. His breathing increased, and his agitation became obvious as he shifted his weight rhythmically from one foot to the other. "You are a bad surgeon. Go back and fix the mess you made. I don't want him shitting into a bag for the rest of his life."

The surgeon's eyes betrayed fear as Quan advanced towards him. The surgeon backed up as far as he could but was against a corner. Quan made a fist in both hands, and before the surgeon could protect himself, Quan was pounding him in the face. He shouted at the top of his lungs, "You are a bad doctor. Go fix him!"

When the surgeon fell to the floor, Quan straddled his chest and continued to hit his face. He was panting. There was blood pouring out of the surgeon's nose, and he had lost consciousness. Rebecca and some of the younger family members pulled Quan off the surgeon. Quan, out of breath, stood staring at the bloody mess he had created. He gave one last kick to the abdomen, then turned around and walked out of the room. The rest of the family quickly followed.

A few days later, Rebecca was in the local farmer's market. She was choosing leeks for a soup she would make for dinner. A man about Rebecca's height was staring at her. She ignored him at first and went to pay for the leeks. He stood in a line behind her after choosing some oranges for himself. Rebecca walked out the door onto the busy street. The man was walking right beside her but kept looking straight ahead. He spoke to her, but his lips didn't move. He said, "I can help you and your family." The man passed his business card to her and said, "Ask Quan to call me." Then he was gone.

Rebecca looked down at the card. There was a number and a website. There was no name. When Rebecca arrived at Quan's house where she was staying, she opened her laptop. She tried the website, but there was a message saying the website did not exist. She tried different browsers, but she still could not access the website.

"Something strange happened at the farmer's market today," said Rebecca at dinner that evening. "A man approached me and gave me this business card." She passed the card to Quan. "He seemed to know you because he said for you to call him."

Quan looked at the card. One side was blank, the other had a phone number and a website. "This website is one from the dark web," said Quan. "It has a dot onion address. I have a Cyber-ghost VPN and software that should get me onto the website. I use this to do business that I don't want the government to know about. It is a secure way to do business. The usual search engines will not find these sites."

After dinner, the 6 family members and Rebecca huddled around Quan's computer. Quan found the website in less than a minute. There was a picture of the surgeon that had operated on his father. He was riding a bicycle on the road. Another picture showed the same surgeon in a hospital bed with bandages wrapped around his face. Underneath that picture was a caption. "The police are looking for the perpetrator to put him in jail." There was a link that said, "services provided." Quan clicked on that link. The list was short. "Permanent solutions offered from $50,000. Call for a quote."

Quan turned to face the rest of the family. "I think I might be in trouble with the police. An investigator visited the house yesterday. The police officer said there were no witnesses, but the surgeon had finished operating on dad. We were the last ones he saw. He asked if I knew anything about the beating. He was waiting until the surgeon was in a strong enough condition to give a statement. I don't want to go to jail."

Rebecca took over the conversation. "Let me talk to this guy. He already approached me in the street. If things go south, I can fly back to Canada, away from Chinese authorities. I'll make certain that whatever it is he has in mind involves none of you. Can we raise $50,000?"

Quan nodded in agreement. "On the dark web, the safest currency is cryptocurrency. It is untraceable. I have enough in my digital wallets to cover the cost. Make the call from a burner phone so no one can trace the call back to you."

The following day, Rebecca purchased a burner phone. She called the number on the card. Someone answered the phone but didn't speak. Rebecca was the first to talk and said, "we want the permanent solution."

There was silence on the other end for 10 seconds before a man spoke. "I am texting you my banking information about where to send the cryptocurrency. This will be our last phone call. Send the transfer tonight. Once I see the transfer has taken place, I will ensure he will not speak with the police. Do not expect a permanent solution to occur for a few weeks. It must look like an accident." Then the phone went dead.

Quan transferred the cryptocurrency as directed by the instructions sent to the burner phone. For the next few weeks, nothing happened. Rebecca and Quan went back to the dot onion website they had visited a few weeks earlier, only to find it no longer existed. When they called the number on the card, a message informed them that the number was not assigned and advised them to check the number and dial again. There had been no further visits from the police to Quan's house.

A few weeks later, there was a news item that started with a video of a mangled bicycle. Quan and the rest of the family diligently watched the news every night to see if there was anything to report about the surgeon. A male reporter said breathlessly, "His bicycle left the overpass and crashed on the street below. The police are informing the family before they release the victim's name." The camera focused on the road that was 30 feet above the mangled bicycle. "Witnesses say he lost control of the bicycle and flew over the guardrail." There was a crowd around the news reporter. In the second row of onlookers was a man about Rebecca's height. Rebecca recognized him as the one who approached her in the farmer's market.

It took Rebecca a month to find him. She applied to be a volunteer at the hospital, hoping to run into him. She placed an ad in the local newspaper that simply said, "For a permanent solution, call 137 4456 9872," hoping to catch his attention. The burner phone received no phone calls or messages for the entire month. Rebecca went back to the farmer's market daily to look for him. She spent some time in the surgical waiting room, hoping he would approach a grieving family. There was no sign of him. He was a ghost.

The Complication

As Rebecca was coming back from a late-night shift from her volunteering job at the hospital, a black car pulled beside her. The window rolled down, and a voice said, "Hop in." She recognized the man as the one with the permanent solution. Rebecca opened the door and sat in the passenger seat as he sped away.

"You were looking for me?" he asked.

"I have a business proposal," said Rebecca.

That was the beginning of her successful business in China. Her cousins would be on the lookout for families or patients that had complications or death resulting from surgical misadventure. They would crisscross the country, using the high-speed train system, never spending more than a week in any city. Jessica, Rebecca's cousin, had devised a system to find clients.

The first time she tried it, Jessica met with her friend Qin, on the surgical floor of the 2000-bed hospital in Qiqihar. They had gone to high school together. "I am the only nurse for 30 patients until 7 AM," complained Qin. "The only relief I get is because most have families that stay all night to help. "That's why I am here," said Jessica. "I can run down to the cafeteria and get you hot tea. I can keep your spirits up by telling you jokes!" They were sitting at the empty nurses' station. It was after midnight, and Qin had finished making her rounds. They were sipping on the hot tea that Jessica had brought from the cafeteria.

"How do you manage angry families and patients at night when there is no one else around?" asked Jessica.

"Sometimes I have to call the doctor," replied Qin. "Then, usually, the doctor will be angry with me for waking him up. I have become used to getting yelled at. I do my best to remain calm, and I try to settle them down."

"Look," said Jessica, "my family offers a support service for angry families and patients through difficult times. We have an answering service available 24 hours a day. The next time an angry family confronts you, give them this number." Jessica handed Qin a stack of business cards.

"There are two families right now who gave me a hard time earlier this evening," said Qin. "Let me give them the number."

Jessica glanced around the nursing station to make sure there was no one who could hear what she was about to say. Seeing no one within earshot, she said, "If any of the families sign up for our services, we will pay you $200."

"Wow!" exclaimed Qin. "I only get $100 for the entire shift. That's double what I would make in a night!"

Within a week, they had signed up two families. Within the first year, they had signed up 100. They also offered their 'eye for an eye, tooth for a tooth' service. If a patient wanted to punish the surgeon for doing an amputation, they would offer to do the same thing to the surgeon. Most of the time, however, the surgeon would meet his end with what appeared to be an accident.

The confidential contact system they used was the same one they used to deal with the surgeon who operated on their grandfather. They would invite the clients to view a specific website on the dark web. Once viewed and money paid, they would eliminate the website. They often would avoid a face-to-face encounter with the family by using a courier service to deliver the contact information.

Rebecca did a google search. She found that in China, there are 4.4 million licensed physicians. That first year, 100 of them died accidentally. No one noticed. Of the $5 million that filled Rebecca's digital wallets, half of the money went to the man who orchestrated the accident. He now had a team of 4 that would help. The other half would stay with Rebecca and her 10 cousins who were involved. They offered beatings at a reduced rate of $10,000. Some clients who wanted the 'eye for an eye, a tooth for a tooth' service, would pay a little more.

The business continued to grow, and last year the number of accidents went to almost 500. Building on the success in China, Rebecca was trying to set up a similar system in Toronto. The biggest problem she faced was the transparency and public accountability of accidents. For example, they would often hold inquests whenever a system problem arose when an accident occurred to find solutions to prevent it from happening again. That is why it was so important for her to control events in her position in the Ontario Ministry of Health.

That is why she needed her lover, Nigel, to get the job as the Deputy Minister of Health.

Chapter 15

Hans stroked his beard as he listened to John recount the events of the past week. "What bothers me most," said John, "is the attitude of Nigel, our chief of staff. It is as if he will select the scenario that best suits his personal goals. It doesn't matter to him what the truth is."

Hans sat back in his chair after hearing the story. "That Nigel would publicly criticize you in front of one million TV viewers is alarming. He demonstrates several characteristics of narcissistic personality disorder, including a lack of empathy, a sense of entitlement, a grandiose sense of self, interpersonal exploitative behavior, and arrogance, to name a few. In your current situation, I would expect the chief of staff to offer support to the chief of surgery rather than publicly admonish you. Has he spoken to you about this directly?"

"He called me many times, and I have yet to answer," said John. "I think he wants me to step down as chief. I am trying to avoid him. I spoke with Nancy, our CEO, who is concerned about the deaths of Joe and Derek. She does not understand how they could change a coroner's report. I think she believed me when I told her something sinister was going on. Do you think I am being paranoid?"

"Paranoia is an unjustified suspicion or mistrust of other people or their actions," said Hans. "In your case, you spoke to the pathologist who felt someone strangled Joe. Now the pathologist is dead. Rick threatened you and said someone paid him to harm you. I would say you are definitely justified in your mistrust of other people and their actions. I would advise you to continue to be careful because something is going on. The truth will eventually come out, and I want you to be around when it does."

John thought about this for a moment. "What do you think I should do? Should I meet with Nigel? Answer his calls?"

"Let me think about that for a moment," responded Hans. "Changing the subject, how are things on the Marie front?"

John went quiet for a few seconds before speaking. "I hoped that wouldn't come up in this hour session." John told Hans about coming home to find Marie in the kitchen with her younger German friend. He told him about finding the separation papers left for him on the kitchen counter. "She said she wants me to sign right away so she can get on with her life. She told me I don't need a lawyer and we can settle this among ourselves."

"What is in the separation papers?" asked Hans.

John sighed. "The house is hers, she says, and it will be up to me to continue to pay the mortgage. She wants $15,000 per month to maintain her in the same living standard. She says the kids will stay with her, and I will pay child support. Marie says I am unfit to look after the kids. Why would she say something like that? I love my kids as much as she does."

"She sounds angry," said Hans.

"I have always treated her well," said John. "I worship the ground she walks on. I have said nothing derogatory to her. Even when she is yelling at me, I remain calm and try to reason with her. It seems to make her angrier, though. I cannot understand what she wants. We have created a life together few have dreamed about. With two wonderful children, we have a bright future. We should strengthen the life we built, not tear it apart."

John shook his head. There was sadness in his voice as he talked. The familiar chest pain and abdominal discomfort returned. He could feel his pulse race. This session was making him anxious, and he had a burning desire to run out of the room. This session was not working for him.

Hans stroked his beard while he spoke. "I am sure you have heard of the '7-year itch.' This occurs when one or both partners become overwhelmed with the feeling that there is more to life than what they are experiencing. This sometimes occurs often when there is a perceived imbalance in the relationship. I suspect Marie doesn't appreciate you putting her on a pedestal. Maybe she feels she has done nothing to deserve that. She might feel you are simply patronizing her. She sees you in an elevated social position as a prominent surgeon and now chief. There is a perceived huge imbalance in the relationship that has occurred. She may feel of lesser value, and that makes her angry. Perhaps she feels there is little she can do to improve her self-worth. The only solution she has come up with is to leave the relationship."

John stared at Hans. He could feel his anxiety resolving as Hans offered him an explanation. There wasn't much he could do about his work as a surgeon. He loved his job. He could do without the job of being the chief, though. The chief of surgery position was turning out to be the source of much of his anxiety. "What can I do to fix this?" John asked.

"It would take the two of you to fix this," responded Hans. "I doubt she is in the frame of mind to change right now. In the meantime, I suggest you meet with the lawyer. My advice would be to proceed slowly and avoid signing anything until things have settled somewhat. As a surgeon, you train to act instinctively and often to react impulsively. You are very good at that, and that is the reason you are such a talented surgeon. This is not the time to be impulsive. There is too much going on for you to make rational decisions."

"Great advice, Hans," said John. "I booked a sailing holiday in Antigua for 10 days beginning next week. Marie was supposed to come but canceled. Another couple is coming. I received a call last night from a sailor who sails with me regularly, named Suzie, who wants to come along. Consequently, all three cabins are now occupied. I need the holiday to think about things."

"I think it would be good for you to get away," said Hans. "Regarding that meeting with Nigel, I think you should meet with him. He cannot strip you of your chief of surgery title. Only the Medical Advisory Committee can do that. Although he is the chair of the Medical Advisory Committee, I doubt he would get sufficient support among the rest of the chiefs to strip you of your chief position."

"I'll meet with him tomorrow then," said John. The chest pain and abdominal discomfort had disappeared. His pulse had settled back to normal. There was no longer the feeling that he had the urge to race out of the office. John felt glad he had spent this time with Hans. It had soothed his spirit. He felt confident he could deal with anything. "I feel much better after spending this hour with you, so thank you!"

"Have a wonderful holiday. I'll see you when you come back," said Hans. John got up and shook Hans' hand before he left the office. Hans had a worried expression on his face as he watched

John walk to his car through his office window. He couldn't help but wonder whether John was next on the hit list and whether he would even see him again. He wondered if there was anything he should do to prevent something bad from happening to John. Everything discussed in the sessions was confidential, so it prevented Hans from saying anything.

John was on his own.

Chapter 16

John spent the next day in the operating room. He was with a 4th-year surgical resident, Sarah. They had just finished their last case, a laparoscopic hernia repair.

"Nice job Sarah," said John. "We consider laparoscopic hernia repair an advanced laparoscopic procedure. We have the entire operation on video, so we can review it with the other residents this afternoon at 4 pm."

Sarah was beaming. "That is the first time I have done the entire operation from skin to skin. Before today, I had only done parts of the procedure. Thank you, Dr. Hegland."

John reflected on her surgery. Her talent as a surgeon shone through. She was precise in her movements. She never hesitated and would skillfully advance to the next step of the operation. John noted she completed the surgery at a similar time as if he were doing the surgery. Although he thought he had taught her well, he knew the real reason she did a great job. She was naturally gifted, and that had nothing to do with him. He looked forward to reviewing her surgery with her this afternoon at the video review rounds to point out all the excellent maneuvers she performed.

As he was walking out of the operating room, his phone binged showing there was an email. He opened the email.

"There is an emergency meeting of the Medical Advisory Committee Meeting tomorrow at 6 PM to discuss the suspension of Dr. John Hegland, the current chief of surgery. Please respond whether you can attend."

John stopped walking and looked for a chair to sit down on. He felt faint. He thought back to the meeting earlier in the morning with Nigel, the chief of staff.

John had arrived at the hospital at 7 AM and went straight to Nigel's administrative office. He was sitting at his desk when John knocked and asked if he could come in.

"I've been trying to reach you, but you are not answering the phone or returning my messages," said Nigel.

"Well," said John, "I'm here now. Let's talk."

"Please," said Nigel cordially, "have a seat."

John took a vacant seat opposite Nigel and sat down. "I'd like to talk with you about how you have been handling the case involving Joe Sawchuk. It was inappropriate of you to go to the coroner's office. That is an enormous breach of patient care, getting confidential information about someone who is not your patient. Second, you had the opportunity to intervene and help him after the complication occurred, but you let him slip back to the bottle. I hold you responsible for his death. Third, you had no right to go to the police precinct and report the death as strangulation. That is the hospital business, and you should have left it up to the hospital to manage its own business. The damage and embarrassment you have caused are insurmountable. I have reported your activities to the College of Physicians and Surgeons. I spoke with their head of the discipline committee, and he agrees you will probably get your license to practice suspended after an appropriate investigation."

John listened incredulously. Nigel had twisted everything around. After thinking about what he was going to say, John responded.

"The coroner was my friend. As chief of surgery, I have spoken many times to the coroner about a death when it was not me who looked after the patient. That is not a breach of confidentiality when I am doing my job as chief.

"Second, Joe had not been drinking. His death was no accident. Someone strangled him and crushed his larynx. Someone, maybe it was you, changed the pathology report to reflect it was an accident and alcohol was involved.

"Third, I went to the precinct for the first time because someone had threatened me. The second time I went to see them was after they killed Derek. That was no accident either. I was there and saw the whole thing happen. It was then that I discussed the autopsy findings that Derek had told me.

"The question I have for you, Nigel, is why are you doing this? Manipulating the media by throwing me under the bus. You know the truth will come out eventually, so why don't you get on board now and save yourself future embarrassment? I know what is going on here, Nigel. I just don't know why you are trying to cover things up."

Nigel's face went red, and the veins in his forehead were bulging. "You cannot hold me responsible for your paranoia!" he screamed. "Get some professional help! Now get the fuck out of here. I won't listen to any more of your bullshit!"

John stood up and calmly said to Nigel, "You always try to bully your way through these situations. It's not going to work this time, Nigel." John turned around, closed the door, and walked away.

While John sat there, he collected his thoughts. He expected Nigel to retaliate, but not this quickly, and not this viciously. John called his medical protective association to get some legal advice. There was an emergency number, which he dialed and left a message. They probably wouldn't get back to him until morning.

John reviewed the mid-term suspension policy. The hospital had a week to hold a hearing. The doctor undergoing suspension could have a lawyer present, but the lawyer could not speak at the hearing. If the doctor disagreed with the Medical Advisory Committee's decision, the doctor could appeal to the board of directors for an independent hearing within a week. In large letters, it stated that no one could discuss the matter with anyone else before the hearing. John suspected this was to maintain integrity and fairness.

Maybe he was getting a little paranoid, John thought. Something didn't seem right when he saw the chief of radiology and chief of medicine having lunch together earlier in the day. They were talking in quiet whispers when he walked by the table where they were sitting. As soon as they saw him, they stopped talking. John greeted them, but they just glared back at him, saying nothing. A thought flashed through his mind then that maybe they found out about the fight he had with Nigel that morning. He quickly dismissed the thought because neither of the two chiefs would get to the hospital before 9 AM, and his meeting with Nigel was much earlier.

After the email notification of the proposed meeting, John was now certain that Nigel had spoken with them to garner support to suspend him. Nigel would have called the meeting only after having certainty for enough votes. That he had spoken with all the chiefs was indisputable the more John thought about it. He would have undoubtedly told them to keep their discussion confidential. John knew if he questioned anyone, that would be further proof he harbored the paranoia that Nigel had accused him of having.

Things did not look promising, thought John.

Chapter 17

John was sitting in a small office down the hall from the boardroom. The Medical Advisory Committee hearing had just taken place. After hearing what John had to say, they asked him to leave while they deliberated. John was sitting with his lawyer, Tracy Davenport. She was shaking her head as she spoke.

"In all my years working with arrogant doctors, I have never seen such a disturbing character as Nigel. He was really enjoying listening to himself. It actually surprised me when he gave you an opportunity to say anything. He has convinced himself that he is smarter than anyone else in the room. The only one in the room that didn't seem in awe of him was you."

John smiled. "Do not underestimate my colleagues. It might frighten them when they think of the power Nigel has over them, but they know what is going on here. Nigel is attempting to bully them. These quiet, sensible medical leaders are used to gentle discussions when differences of opinion occur. They balance the pros and cons of a rational argument. They do not know how to manage an intimidating, ebullient person in power, such as Nigel. Throwing me down the suspension path is telling the chiefs he will do the same to them if they disagree with him. I am prepared for the inevitable outcome of this meeting."

John thought about a call he received last night. The president of the medical staff association, Jamie Spritz, tried to call him. John was sitting in his home office reviewing what he was going to say at the hearing. He was about to say goodnight to his kids when he got the call. John declined the call but sent him a text message instead.

"I assume you are calling to find out how I am doing. I am fine. After reviewing the mid-term suspension policy, it clearly states we may not discuss among ourselves, so the process remains impartial and fair. Can we discuss it after the meeting tomorrow? I do not want to be accused of tainting the process. Thanks for your understanding."

"You have great integrity. I was not aware of that. Maybe someone should have explained that to Nigel……" was the response.

John read the message twice. This confirmed his suspicion that Nigel had, in fact, tainted the process by discussing the meeting with the chiefs. Prior to the hearing, John had discussed the implications with Tracy, but because she could say nothing at the meeting, she suggested waiting for the outcome before challenging the integrity of the process.

John thought about something else his daughter had said to him last night. He knocked on her door to find her in the usual position in front of the computer.

"Dad, I went back to that website where your name appeared, you know, the one we looked at before, and it no longer exists. That worries me. On the dark web, when there is disturbing content, after the messaging finishes, they will dismantle the site. I wanted to find out more, but I can't now. You need to be careful."

"Honey," said John, "you are worried about something that no longer exists? My senses tell me to be relieved."

"Dad, how could you get through life by being so naïve?" asked Ainslie, shaking her head. "I don't want anything bad to happen to you. Mom is never around anymore. You are all Claudia and I have."

"Don't worry," answered John. "I will be very careful. I love you both and I want nothing bad to happen to me either. Next week, I am going away for ten days, sailing. Last chance to change your mind and come along. No? OK then, do not drive grandma and grandpa crazy. I have instructed them not to spoil you."

"Dad," sighed Ainslie. "Why do you always treat me like a child? I'm grown up."

"You'll always be my little baby," said John as he kissed her on the top of her head. "Don't stay up late."

John went back to his office and thought about what Ainslie had said about the dark website. He could not relate to the significance, but something about the site rattled her. Although she was only 12 years old, she had a good understanding of how things worked in the world. He felt so out of touch with these kinds of things compared to her.

There was a knock on the office door, snapping John out of his reverie. Mary, the assistant taking the minutes of the meeting, was at the door.

"They are ready to see you in the boardroom," she said.

John and Tracy got up and walked the few steps to the boardroom. They sat in the seats they had previously used. The room was quiet. Nigel spoke to John in a triumphant tone.

"After much deliberation, the Medical Advisory Committee has voted to suspend your privileges in view of your past indiscriminate behavior, which we feel is unprofessional. The suspension is to take effect immediately. Your lawyer will advise you of your right to appeal to the board.

Tracy stood up. She could barely control the anger. In a quavering voice, she spoke.

"I know I am not allowed to speak at this hearing, but this entire process has been a sham." She stared around at the chiefs who tried to escape her stare by looking down at the papers in front of them. "You in this room should be ashamed of yourselves. The master of intimidation has intimidated you. You should know that the truth will come out about what happened to Joe Sawchuk, and I will hold you all accountable for not acting responsibly."

She turned to Nigel. "You have tainted the process by speaking with the chiefs ahead of time to garner support for suspending John. I will hold you accountable for that. You are on notice that we are appealing this decision to the board of directors, as is our right in the bylaws. It seems I need to remind you about the process. As chief of staff, as outlined in the bylaws, you must not discuss with anyone from the board ahead of time. I want you to know I am watching you."

Nigel's face went red, and the veins on his forehead bulged. His eyes glared back at the diminutive female lawyer, the only one tonight, other than John, who dared to challenge him. She glared back at him, stood up, and tapped John on the shoulder. John and Tracy left the room together.

Chapter 18

The sun beat down on John's back; it was already 28 degrees Celsius, although it was only 9 AM. John checked the life raft attached to the stern rail of the 46-foot sailboat owned by the Antigua charter company, Happy Days. Everything seemed in order, and it was not due for evaluation by the safety team until next September. John reviewed the emergency instructions written on the casing. There were two pins that needed detachment to launch the life raft into the water, where it would self-inflate. It was a 6-person life raft equipped with a manual water maker, flares, fishing tackle, and other safety gear. John also had a 'ditch bag' containing a spare GPS, Garmin In Reach device, flashlights, spare batteries, and dried packages of energy powder. He knew from experience that you could not have too much safety equipment on board.

A few years earlier, John had purchased a beautiful sailboat in Greece. He and Marie had flown to Athens and rented a car to drive to the Ionian coast. The sailboat had been owned by an ageing Brit, who had to sell because of health problems. She was a beautiful Beneteau 45-foot sailboat designed for cruising and only 2 years old. She had all the equipment available for ocean sailing, including a water maker, generator, radar, freezers, and all the necessary safety equipment for a safe passage. Their plan was to sail on Lake Ontario during the summers instead of having a cottage like many of their friends. John smiled as he reflected on that trip to Greece with Marie. They had big plans to keep their marriage exciting and full. How things can change, thought John.

John found a delivery skipper and crew who had a great reputation for successful transatlantic crossings. Randy Murdock delivered hundreds of boats during his 30-year career as a delivery skipper. For $200 a day, he said it would take 30 days for the 5000-mile passage to Toronto. John followed him on the Marine tracking app from the safety of his cellphone in Toronto, as Randy made his way across the Mediterranean and then south along the African coast. Crossing the Atlantic, Randy successfully dodged several storms until he got within 200 miles of Nova Scotia. With winds reaching 55 knots, the waves were enormous. The steering broke, and the sails shredded in the brutal winds. The three crew members feared for their lives as the tempest tossed them around mercilessly. Randy placed a mayday call using his satellite radio.

The Canadian Coast Guard dispatched a helicopter to rescue them. The helicopter refueled at the Hibernia oil rig, 200 miles off the coast of Newfoundland, then left to rescue the distressed sailors. As the sailboat was getting battered by the waves, the pilot felt it was not safe to lower a rescue basket onto the deck of the bouncing sailboat, so he instructed them to launch their life raft to be rescued from the open ocean. Randy went to the stern of the boat and released the pins holding the raft to the plastic case. The raft flew out of the casing and self-inflated. The wind was so powerful, the life raft tore the railing from the stern of the boat, so it was no longer attached. Randy watched as the life raft went flipping head over heels as it became airborne. Within seconds, the life raft disappeared on the horizon as if swallowed by the storm.

With darkness approaching, the pilot knew he would have to take the chance that the rigging of the sailboat would not get wrapped up with the rescue gear and pull the helicopter into the raging ocean. Carefully, they lowered the basket with the rescuer onto the deck of the sailboat. One by one, he pulled the sailors to safety. Randy was the last of the sailors to get pulled to safety. The last image Randy had of John and Marie's dream was from 500 feet above the water as the helicopter flew them back to the base in Halifax and to the safety of the land.

That was the beginning of the end of their marriage, thought John. The stress of losing their dream was too much for Marie to bear. She saw this as a sign as to where their marriage was heading. They argued about trivial matters and slept in separate rooms. When John booked the 10-day sailing adventure 6 months earlier, he hoped it would revitalize their marriage. He hoped the magic of the ocean would soothe their differences and piece their fractured spirits back together. John sighed as he now realized it was too much to hope for.

John, with the rest of his crew, arrived in Antigua the night before. It was dark when the security guard gave them the keys to their rented 2022 Beneteau sailboat. They planned to circumnavigate the island and spend 1 or 2 days in Barbuda to visit the bird sanctuary there. The four of them were planning on doing a lot of scuba diving, snorkeling, and exploring.

Bev and Debbie were the married couple of the crew. They had chosen the cabin at the front of the boat because it had a queen-sized bed and its own head. They were all familiar with washrooms being called 'heads' on sailboats. The origin was not entirely clear, but seemed to have arisen from the golden days of sailing, when sailors would crawl onto the netting at the front of the sailing vessel to do their business. They would rely on the waves to wash away the stool with mixed results.

Bev had been sailing with John over the past 10 years. He was in his early 30s of Hispanic origin. He pulled his thick black hair into a ponytail. His face had angular features because of keeping in top shape with less than 5% body fat. He prided himself on his muscular body by running 10 kilometers daily and spending at least 1 hour in the gym working out. He worked in IT at the same hospital as John. His wife Debbie had been working on her PhD in biochemistry for the past 5 years. She had short, blond hair cut as a bob framing a pretty face. She was petite, weighing 100 lbs. They shared their love of the ocean and perpetually looked forward to holidays in the south. This was the first time they had been to Antigua.

Suzie was the last crew member on the sailboat. She had been sailing with John for the last 3 seasons on Lake Ontario. She originated from Colombia, having moved to Toronto for work 6 years ago. At 28 years old, she spoke English with a slight Spanish accent. She was a schoolteacher, but also had a master's degree in psychology and doubled as the school psychologist. She piled up her long jet-black curly hair in a bun on the top of her head to prevent it from getting tangled in the trade winds. Getting time off work was challenging. Typically, she had agreed to take time off work during the usual school holidays, but she convinced her boss that because she had to work a few extra days during the Christmas holidays and March break, this entitled her to at least 10 days off during the school year. For her, spending 10 days on a sailboat in Antigua was a dream come true.

"What are you doing?" asked Suzie as she climbed out of the main salon, rubbing her eyes. She had just woken up.

"I am checking the safety stuff with the hope we will not use it," answered John. "Everything seems in good shape. We won't be more than a few miles from the land, anyway."

"Bev and Debbie are still unconscious," said Suzie. "I was going to go shopping for food. Do you want to come along?"

There were only a few large grocery stores in Antigua. One was a block away from the marina. They needed enough food and drinks for 10 days. There were many hotels and restaurants across the island, but many of the nights, they hoped to be isolated in remote anchorages, away from the crowds of tourists. They were all scuba divers and had brought their own equipment, so they planned to dive on the reefs. The charter company provided 8 tanks, and there was a list of places where they could fill their scuba tanks as they made their way around the island. The sailboat had large freezers, fridges, and storage for supplies. There was a water maker to turn seawater into freshwater, and an ice maker.

"Sure," said John, "let me grab the list we made last night." He went into his cabin and returned with the list of food they had agreed upon and his wallet. "Let's go."

They walked in silence as the morning sun warmed them. There was a gentle breeze coming off the sea, which cooled them. There were a few fair-weather puffy clouds over the hilltops. The hills were green with thick vegetation, and there was a pleasant smell of flowers coming off the land. As John walked down the dusty road in this paradise, he thought about the contrast with his disrupted life at home.

The Medical Advisory Committee suspended him last week. He spent the rest of the week preparing for the board of directors meeting, which would take place the Monday after returning to Toronto. He was having difficulty understanding how his life could unravel so quickly. Tracy, his lawyer, had convinced John he had done nothing wrong, and all his actions were reasonable. She could not understand why this draconian path of suspension had occurred, except to feed the enormous ego of the chief of staff. John agreed it was the continuous conflict between him and Nigel that led to the suspension. John knew that once Nigel had enough votes to get his suspension, he organized the meeting and bullied his colleagues into agreeing with him.

There must be more to this than Nigel's ego driving him, John thought as they entered the grocery store.

Chapter 19

"I just got a strange text message," said Suzie as they were leaving the grocery store. Suzie had a concerned look on her face as she looked at her phone. She put down the bags of groceries to look at the text message. "It's from your daughter, Ainslie. She wants you to call her right away, but she says not to use your phone and to ask if you can use mine." Suzie showed the message to John.

John looked at the message and shrugged his shoulders. "Why doesn't she just call me? She knows I have my phone on me. What is she doing up so early? Usually on weekends, she doesn't get up until noon."

"Just call her," said Suzie.

John had to look up her cellphone number on his phone before punching in Ainslie's number. Ainslie picked up on the first ring. "Dad, you've been hacked!" cried Ainslie.

"What are you talking about, honey?" asked John.

"I went on the dark web and checked out your name," said Ainslie. "All your email addresses are there, along with all the passwords you have used in the past 5 years. You need to take a course in cybersecurity, dad. You used my birthday as a password! What were you thinking? Anyway, I called your phone, and it went to a generic voice message. Your usual message with your voice was not there. You need to call your cell provider, AT&T, to find out what happened. I think someone has stolen your identity."

John went silent for a moment then said, "Ok pumpkin. I'm sure it is just because I'm in the Caribbean, and the cell coverage is not as good."

"Dad!" cried Ainslie. "What is the matter with you? This is serious. Call me back after you have spoken with them. Also, you need to call Equifax and TransUnion to find out if your credit rating has changed. You can get their numbers online."

"What is Equifax and TransUnion, and how do you know all this?" asked John.

"Dad," said Ainslie. "We study cybersecurity in school. The rest I have picked up browsing the internet."

"How did you get Suzie's number?" asked John.

Ainslie sighed, "Dad, I used the password that is on the dark web to access your email account. You need to switch over to 2-step authentications. Anyway, Suzie has her cell number with her email address. You should cancel all your credit cards immediately and change your passwords on Facebook and Instagram. Change your bank passwords as well."

"Will do," said John. "What are you doing up so early?"

Ainslie responded with stony silence. John said, "You haven't been to bed yet, have you?"

More silence greeted John on the other end of the phone. Then she said, "Bye dad. Call me back when you have spoken with AT&T. I love you." Ainslie hung up before John could respond.

By the time Suzie and John got back to the boat, Bev and Debbie were sitting in the cockpit drinking coffee in paper cups. "We got some coffee and bagels at the marina. It was free! Do you want me to get you some?" asked Bev.

"We have enough coffee to last for 2 weeks, so I'll get started on a pot now," said John. "Bev, you work at the hospital in IT. According to my daughter, someone hacked into my accounts and stole my identity. She tried to call my phone, and they forwarded it to a voicemail that wasn't mine."

"That is classic identity theft," said Bev. "That way, whenever a credit card company or AT&T calls, the thief can intercept the call. It might involve a transaction, or it might be used to confirm the origin of a request."

"How does a thief get my calls forwarded to his phone?"

"There are a variety of ways, but he'll use their security system to his favor," explained Bev. "Let's say he calls AT&T and reveals to them he is away from his computer but wants to make a payment on his bill. The operator tells him he owes, let's say, $52. He then says he wants to forward his messages to his new phone because he is in the US and left his phone at home. The operator then sends his call to a different department. After the usual 1 to 2 hours wait, someone comes to his phone. One of the security questions could be to tell the new operator the outstanding amount on the last bill. Having the correct answer, AT&T will now forward all phone calls to his phone."

"How does he get my cellphone number?" asked John.

"Maybe he bought the information, along with your email information and passwords, on the dark web," suggested Bev. "Maybe he just came across it the same way as your daughter. Let's check your credit cards."

John turned on his computer and, using his cellphone as a hotspot, he connected to American Express. He ran through his latest transactions. "Holy shit," he exclaimed. "There's a $32,000 purchase for bitcoin done yesterday!"

"Let's put a hold on the credit card while you call them," suggested Bev.

John made a call to AmEx. They answered the call after running through the menu to direct him to the correct department.

John said to the person who answered, "There's a purchase for $32,000 for bitcoin, that I never made."

"Hmmm," said the operator. "It says here they called you before agreeing to the transaction, and you confirmed the purchase."

John explained the problem he was having with the phone. "If that wasn't you, I suggest you call your cellphone provider and get that part fixed. We need to confirm that this is really you before we refund the money. What are the last 4 digits on your account?"

John immediately became suspicious. "Hang on," he said. "You should know that! How do I know you are not the one scamming me again?"

"You are the one who called us; don't forget," said the operator politely. "I can understand you being a little paranoid, but you need to understand that we must confirm it is you we are speaking with and not the perpetrator."

John sighed. For the next hour, they ran through a series of questions. They bounced him up the hierarchy chain to the supervisor, and the supervisor asked a series of questions. They told him to file a police report, and they canceled the American Express credit card. John logged onto his bank and went through the rest of his credit cards. There were no unusual purchases. He changed his passwords and enabled the 2-step verification process to access his accounts.

The next call was to AT&T. It was 1 hour before someone got to the phone. John explained the problem he was having with the voicemail going to a phone that was not his.

"That's weird," said the operator. "It's probably the cell service in Antigua. It can be a little spotty down south."

John was reaching levels of frustration, making it hard for him to remain civil. "Look!" he shouted. "I have been on the phone for the past 4 hours. Someone bought $32,000 of bitcoin using my American Express card yesterday. Amex told me they called my number, and someone, not me, confirmed the purchase. Someone had my phone forwarded to their number. Now, give me your supervisor!"

There was silence on the other end. John could hear the clicks of a keyboard as the operator was checking something. "Oh my God," he exclaimed. "I remember this call. It was yesterday, and he knew all the security questions, including the account balances. The only thing he was uncertain was which email account belonged to the cellphone account. I am so sorry. We'll reverse the call forwarding immediately. I'll put you to my supervisor."

After finishing the call with the supervisor, John called Ainslie. "Hello," she answered sleepily.

"Hi, sweetie," said John. "You were right. Someone bought $32,000 of bitcoin with my AmEx card. I've been on the phone for the past 4 hours with the bank, AT&T, and AmEx. I'll call those credit agencies later today so if someone applies for a loan, they know to call me first and confirm. I'll file a police report, too."

"Dad, the police report is a waste of time," said Ainslie, now fully awake. "If AmEx refunds your money, you are no longer the victim, they are. The police get 60,000 fraud calls a year and cannot keep up, so don't waste your time with that. Make sure you change your social media passwords, so they don't post inappropriate material on your behalf."

John thought about that for a minute and said, "Thanks pumpkin, you have no idea how grateful I am having you alert me so quickly. How did you get so smart?

"There is something else," said Ainslie. "There is a website on the dark web with your name again. There is a woman holding a piece of paper. Everything is in Mandarin, but when I translate it into English, it makes no sense. When I click on the paper she is holding, some numbers and letters come up and your name is in the middle. It makes no sense to me. Dad, I am worried. Be careful!"

Just as John hung up, he got a Facebook message saying someone was attempting to log into his account. "Was this you?" the message asked.

John responded with "No". He then went on Facebook and Instagram and changed all his passwords. He enrolled in the 2-step verification as well. John logged onto his Facebook and Instagram accounts and checked for new postings from himself. There were none. He breathed a sigh of relief.

John had spent the morning and the early part of the afternoon on the phone. The plan to sail to Falmouth Harbor would have to wait until tomorrow. The charter company Happy Days operated out of Jolly Harbour, 16 miles northwest of their first stop. John climbed out of the main salon to the cockpit. The two girls were sitting on cushions on the foredeck, drinking white wine. The bottle was sitting in an ice bucket. It was almost empty. John could hear Suzie laugh at something Debbie had said.

"I am so sorry," said John. "We were supposed to anchor in Falmouth Harbor today, but it is too late to leave now. Are you OK if we leave tomorrow?"

The two women stared at John, then burst out laughing. "We are in no condition to go anywhere! We are happy hanging out here. Bev went to the gym to work out for 2 hours. Why don't you crack a beer and tell us all about your identity theft woes?"

John told them about the phone calls. Out of the corner of his eye, he caught the reflection of glass in the sunlight. When he turned to look, the man holding the binoculars pulled them down and stared at John. He was sitting in the driver's seat of a cigarette boat across the other side of the marina. Although John could not be certain because the man was sitting down, he resembled Rick, the man who had threatened him before. The man pointed his finger at John and made like it was a gun pulling a trigger. A chill ran through his body as he stopped talking mid-sentence. When Debbie and Suzie turned to see what John was looking at, the man had disappeared behind the boat's console. They looked up at John with a worried look.

John, who was shaking now, sat down and said, "I think there is another problem we need to talk about before we leave."

Chapter 20

"I need your advice on how to manage this," said Nigel.

He was sitting in a private room in the 5-star restaurant at the Four Seasons Hotel in downtown Toronto. Rebecca was sitting opposite him. The lights were dim, and there was a small candle on the white tablecloth flickering. There was a solitary white rose in a long-stemmed vase next to the candle. Beside them, on a separate table, was the Peking duck ready to be carved. In an ice bucket on a silver stand was a bottle of Krug Champagne Grande Cuvee NV. They were celebrating. They had chosen Nigel as the new Deputy Minister of Health. He beat the other candidates by a wide margin. They chose him because of his ability to get things done, even when there was fierce opposition. In the public health care environment, tough decisions were necessary, but few were capable of making them. Nigel would be the one to lead them to keep the budget on track while maintaining health care services.

"Before we get to that," said Rebecca. "Congratulations!" Rebecca leaned over the table and clinked her champagne glass against his, and they both drank to his success. She leaned over further and planted a kiss on his lips. She slipped her tongue into his mouth. The kiss lasted 10 more seconds before they disengaged. She smiled at him silently while she reflected on how her careful planning had been worthwhile.

"Thanks for your support, Rebecca," said Nigel, as he smiled back at her. "We are in for a great ride. I am supposed to start in a month's time. There are a few things I need to clear up at the hospital before then. The biggest roadblock could be John Hegland, the asshole surgeon I suspended at the Medical Advisory Committee meeting last week. Somehow, his lawyer found out I spoke with the chiefs ahead of time. I needed to make sure I had enough votes. I also told them there would be consequences if they mentioned the conversation to anyone. Someone must have let it slip out that I spoke to them ahead of the meeting. When I checked the medical staff bylaws afterward, it clearly says in bold font not to discuss the meeting ahead of time so that the process remains fair and impartial."

"What do you think could happen, then?" asked Rebecca.

"They have asked for a hearing before the board of directors, which is scheduled in 2 weeks," said Nigel. "If the board feels I tainted the process, then they could toss out the suspension, and me along with it. If that happens, it will cast a dark shadow on my performance as chief of staff. Undoubtedly, this will come back to haunt me later as the Deputy Minister. I cannot allow that to happen."

Rebecca became silent while she thought about what Nigel said. In the world of health care, a fair process was the most important determinant of success. In public office, it was essential to have a completely clean record. Nigel was correct that any hint of inappropriate conduct would haunt him throughout his term as Deputy Minister. He needed to be untouchable by his past. This problem with John Hegland needed to be fixed.

The previous Deputy Minister had a reputation of fairness and honesty. This 5-star reputation evaporated with a single scandal. There was a hospital in Norway where they delivered linen, medical supplies, and food to the hospital wards by robots. They were reliable, never called in sick, and would recharge themselves when the electric battery ran low. They were available 24 hours a day and never complained or wanted extra pay for overtime. He estimated it would save each hospital $2 million per year in salaries that the hospitals could use for direct patient care rather than paying wages to the porters. The unions went ballistic. After the necessary public debate, the Ontario Ministry of Health spent $200 million on the robots that were designed and produced in Norway. The Ontario Ministry of Health distributed the robots to the hospitals that requested them.

The problem came when the unions did a thorough analysis of the Norway meeting. They discovered that there were meals at expensive restaurants, a tour of the majestic Norwegian fjords, and a private tour of Oslo, including dinner and a show, all paid for by the robot company. The unions claimed they had bribed the deputy minister. This made front-page headline news for 3 days in a row. Anything the deputy minister said in his defense, the media ignored. That the deputy minister had refunded the cost of these events to his hosts before leaving Norway simply added fuel to the fire. Now, the media accused him of spending tax dollars on lavish events that the ordinary Canadian citizen could only dream about. What Nigel had done was orders of magnitude worse on the public scrutiny score.

"I have a few thoughts on how to manage this," said Rebecca. "The first step would be to get John to discredit himself so that anything he said is not believed. Imagine what would happen if he posted outrageous things on Facebook and Instagram. This could include personal things about the board members that are false. Consider the possibility of him stating that he had multiple affairs with the female board members and exposing this will lead to his exoneration. If John claimed you tainted the process at the Medical Advisory meeting, no one would believe him. The board will be more concerned about maintaining fairness in their own process."

"Exactly how will you get him to make those false claims?" asked Nigel.

"We'll do it for him," said Rebecca. "It is easy to access his Facebook and Instagram accounts if we have his passwords. We'll port his information from his cellphone, so if there is a 2-step verification, we can intercept it. It typically takes about 6 weeks before anyone figures out someone has hacked them. By that time, the inevitable conclusion of John's career will be over, and they will laud you for taking those tough decisions by suspending him."

Nigel thought about all this as he ate his Peking duck. He washed down a mouthful of delicious duck with the expensive champagne, when a negative thought flashed through his mind. "What if it doesn't work?" he asked. "How can you assure me I am not implicated in his demise? I don't know if this is a good idea. Maybe I should just take my chances that the board believes me and not him. He's trying to save his ass. I'm just doing my job."

"Nigel," answered Rebecca. "Look how quickly the discussion about Joe Sawchuk has ground to a halt since deflecting the blame to his chief, and away from you. The same will happen at the board of directors' meeting. Stealing identities happens 60,000 times a year in Canada. Many of the cases never get reported. There is no way to keep track of every event. It is very easy to steal someone's identity, and no one ever gets caught. The trail is so complex on the dark web, there is no accountability. John won't know what hit him."

They continued with their dinner as they brought more courses to them. The dinner concluded with the most exquisite cheesecake. Cappuccinos and Courvoisier brandy followed dessert.

They discussed their strategies to improve the Ontario Ministry of Health by cutting costs and firing many who they considered deadbeats. They toasted to themselves after talking of success and better days ahead. However, Nigel had a nagging feeling that his problems were not over. He remained dubious about Rebecca's plan. He felt there was too much risk. Rebecca had not convinced Nigel that her plan would work.

"There is still the risk that it won't have the effect that I need to take all the focus away from me," said Nigel. "I need something foolproof."

"I have a Plan B," said Rebecca. "My Plan B is foolproof.

Chapter 21

They were sitting on the stone wall overlooking English Harbour at Shirley Heights, Antigua. The warm trade winds blew in from the east. At 490 feet above sea level, they could see their rented sailboat anchored below them in front of Galleon Beach. It was Sunday evening, and a band was playing soft music. The sun was setting, and at least 50 people were getting in position with their cellphones in hand to catch the spectacular sight to send to their jealous friends back home. There were some thin clouds on the horizon, so when the sun set, the sky turned a brilliant orange and red color. It took another half an hour for darkness to arrive.

John, Bev, and Debbie were drinking Heineken beer. Suzie was drinking white wine. They had enjoyed the barbecued chicken, for which the restaurant was famous. It had been a strenuous climb, sometimes straight up the cliff on the poorly marked path to the top. They decided they would take a taxi back to English Harbour because of the darkness.

Earlier that morning, they set sail from Jolly Harbour. Fortunately, the winds were light, and they had to motor most of the way directly into the easterly trade winds. It took about 2 hours to arrive at English Harbour. They found a suitable spot to anchor close to the beach and spent the morning exploring. After visiting Nelson's Dockyard and Falmouth Harbour, they found themselves in awe of the massive yachts that arrived for the Charter Boat Trade Show they host every year.

"Imagine if we could have rented the largest yacht for $1 million per week," said John as they gazed at the lights of the mega-yachts in the harbor from the top of Shirley Heights.

"I can't imagine I would be happier than I am now," replied Suzie thoughtfully. Bev and Debbie nodded their heads in agreement. "This has been the best trip ever," said Debbie. "We can go where we want anytime. I imagine those massive yachts would require a lot of planning to move them. We, on the other hand, might decide to pull the anchor tomorrow, or we might stay put. I enjoy having that kind of control."

"Maybe tomorrow we can head to Green Island," suggested Bev. "The diving is supposed to be amazing. We can get there in an hour, but we will have to slog our way into the trade winds to get there. On the north side of the island, we should find a suitable spot to anchor. We can dive right from the back of the boat. We would need to leave early to get the best spot."

John smiled as they were talking among themselves. No one appeared spooked after he told them about what had happened to Joe Sawchuk and Derek and their gruesome deaths. He thought back to their conversations after he explained to them everything that had happened over the 2 weeks. They had some theories about why the autopsy report had been changed to reflect an alcohol-related death. If it turned out that he was murdered, Suzie suggested they might hold the hospital responsible for not keeping their doctors safe from angry families. The way things stood now; they left John taking the blame for not reaching out to help Joe. The hospital could now carry on as if nothing had happened.

Debbie suggested that something more sinister was going on, especially since John had received threats on multiple occasions. The last one was yesterday, from that guy across the marina. Bev agreed with his wife there was something more sinister. Bev pointed out that John recovered from the identity theft attempt so quickly only because of a hyper-vigilant and computer-savvy daughter. It might have been weeks before he discovered there was a problem. It was also possible that someone had tried to hack into his Facebook account, and the 2-step verification failed because John's cellphone was no longer forwarded to the thief's number.

They all agreed not to let this ruin their trip of a lifetime but committed to always staying together as a group of four. Safety in numbers was the thinking behind that. They would travel in pairs to the washroom if they were in a restaurant, and never would only one of them go to the store to get something. Bev mentioned that as part of his workout to keep in shape, he would engage in Tae Kwon Do. This is the Korean martial art using kicking and punching, he explained. Bev said the techniques are great to keep flexible and to develop muscles that usual weightlifting exercises miss. He said he has never had to use this to defend himself but would look forward to trying his moves if Rick ever came near enough to him.

The only one who seemed worried was John. Things had spun out of his control. He found it difficult to believe someone was attempting to ruin his life. He wondered if it had something to do with Marie and his impending divorce, but that was too far-fetched. Besides, she would never do anything to disrupt the income flow. There was something going on with Nigel, but it seemed to be a lot of effort on his part. John could not imagine what Nigel would gain by ruining him, except to keep his status as the biggest jerk on the planet.

The band was playing a song from the Village People, "YMCA," and those that had finished eating and had a few drinks got up to dance. They lined themselves up along the stone wall and pantomimed the lyrics, using their arms as letters. Suzie grabbed John's hand, and they both joined the line on the stone wall. A spotlight lit up the dancers. They were singing the lyrics at the top of their lungs with the rest of the group. Surprisingly, no one fell off the stone wall.

The next song was Elton John's 'Crocodile Rock'. The dancers jumped off the stone wall and began swinging each other to the music. John, who had taken rock 'n roll dance lessons in his 20s, still remembered the moves. Suzie responded to his lead, and they even tried a few complex moves, where he swung her over his back. She clearly had taken lessons in a previous life. After the dance had finished, they were out of breath.

"That was great," said John. "I haven't danced like that in years! Thank you."

Suzie leaned over and kissed him on the cheek. "Thank you," she said. A shock went through John like a live electric wire starting on the cheek where she had kissed him and passing through to the bottom of his feet. He stood there, watching her walk back to their table where Bev and Debbie were sitting. She was swaying her hips, and as if sensing he was watching her, turned around and smiled at him. John felt faint but managed to make it back to the table without falling. Bev organized another round of drinks, and they laughed and told stories about their dancing days when they were younger.

As the crowds from Shirley Heights thinned, the four of them called a cab to take them back to their dinghy. The dinghy was where they had left it, chained to a palm tree on the beach. The beach was well lit by the streetlights. They pulled it back into the water, and the 2 women jumped in. Bev sat at the back of the boat, ready to start the engine. He pulled the cord, and the 10 hp engine started on the second try. Bev unhinged the engine, so the shaft and propeller went into the water.

They were ready to head back to the boat. John went up to the beach to retrieve the bags. As he was looking around to see he had everything, there was a shadow that crossed in front of the streetlight. John looked up. Leaning against the palm tree they had used to tie up the dinghy was Rick. There was a sardonic smile on his face. His eyes were dark and piercing. They betrayed not a hint of kindness. He had crossed his legs at his feet as he leaned against the tree. He had a small baton in his left hand and was slapping it onto the palm of his right hand rhythmically. There was a soft popping noise coming from the slapping. He continued to stare at John, not looking away.

John felt a chill run through his body. His heart raced. He felt a cold sweat on his brow, even though it was a warm night. "What do you want?" shouted John. "Keep the fuck away from me!"

Rick smiled and slapped the baton against his hand. The 2 men stared at each other. Fear ran through John as he tried to imagine why Rick was in Antigua and why he was tracking him. It was obvious he was there to intimidate. Would he try to hurt him? What was the purpose? John remained frozen in his place, not sure what to do next, when Rick turned around and started walking away.

Bev, upon hearing the commotion, hopped out of the dinghy. He raced up to the beach to where John was standing. He breathed heavily as Rick walked away from them. The streetlight cast a long shadow. Both John and Bev stared at his back as he slowly made his way down the street. Just as he was about to turn a corner, Rick turned to the two of them and pointed his index finger at them. Using his middle finger, he pulled the trigger as if his hand were a gun. He then turned and walked away.

Chapter 22

The TV screen was fixed to the bulkhead of the boat. The four of them were sitting in the main salon, drinking. Suzie had a glass of wine, while the others opted for beer. They couldn't sleep because of the lingering tension after the encounter with Rick. It was one in the morning. Despite the darkness outside, the images on the TV screen were surprisingly clear.

"I wasn't going to use the cameras, but after tonight and meeting that creep, I feel safer with them running," said Bev. "I have similar cameras in our apartment in Toronto, and no one would even know they were there."

Bev had brought tiny cameras and their small solar panels as carry-on luggage. Bev fixed three of the tiny cameras to the mast, which offered a 360 degree view of the sea around the boat. He hid two in the bimini and dodger, and one looked out from the stern. There was also one on the bow for reef spotting while sailing.

"They work the same as dashboard cameras in cars," said Bev. "We record everything onto my laptop."

"I hope you didn't put any in the bedrooms. My room wouldn't exactly be action-packed," Suzie laughed.

"No worries about privacy," said Bev, smiling. "The other safety feature I added was to electrify the lifelines. The switch to turn it on is just as you enter the main salon on the right." Bev pointed to the wall at the entrance to the main salon from the companionway.

"It is 12 volts," he continued. "Not enough to hurt or kill someone, but enough to scare the daylights out of them. If you hear screaming in the night, don't assume it is coming from me and Deb. It could be an intruder." They all laughed.

"I taped a note to the companionway door to remind us to turn it off when we wake up in the morning," said Bev.

They all breathed a sigh of relief. "I'm ready to go to bed," said Suzie. "I think the wine is finally kicking in."

They bid each other goodnight and went to their cabins. The sailboat rocked gently in the small waves in the protected harbor, making it easy to fall asleep. Within seconds of lying down, John was asleep.

The smell of coffee woke John. He glanced at his watch. It was 7 AM. He felt rested. Sitting alone in the cockpit drinking coffee was Suzie. John went to the Nespresso machine and made a cup of Colombian coffee. He climbed up the companionway and joined Suzie in the cockpit. "How did you sleep?" he asked.

"I slept great," said Suzie. "I turned off the electrified lifeline when I got up. Without that reminder note to turn it off, I could have been the one screaming. I slept so well I forgot about the security concerns."

John smiled, then asked. "Should we get ready to go? I'll start the engine, and you can raise the anchor with the windlass. I'm sure the racket will waken up Bev and Debbie."

John started the engine, checked the ocean for boat traffic, and ensured it was safe to pull up the anchor and leave. As predicted, they would go directly into the trade winds, so there was no need to raise the sails.

"Move a little to starboard," said Suzie into the wireless headphones she was wearing. Suzie pressed the button to raise the anchor on the handheld device connected to the windlass. She was at the bow of the boat and needed headphones to communicate with John, who was at the helm.

"Will do," replied John into his headphones.

John powered up the engine to move the boat to starboard as Suzie raised the anchor. Using the windlass, she pulled the 85 lb. anchor into the cradle on the bowsprit, connected the pin, and made her way back to the cockpit. "We make a good team, you and me," she whispered, while still wearing the headphones.

John looked up at her and smiled while he nodded in affirmation. He turned the boat to head out of the harbor and into the ocean. There were 6-foot waves, and they headed directly into them. The boat would plow into the bottom of the wave, sending spray onto the dodger but also slowing the boat. The erratic movements of the boat brought Bev and Debbie out of their forward cabin, as it was not possible to sleep. They sleepily made their way into the cockpit after deciding it was too rough to make coffee for themselves.

After an hour of the up-and-down motion, Debbie leaned over the rail and vomited. She had never been seasick before. Bev went below to retrieve the anti-nauseant pill, Gravol. She waved him off, saying she was okay, but promptly vomited again.

It took about two hours before they entered the bay and found an anchorage on the north side of Green Island. The sea was calm in the protected waters. Debbie recovered from her seasickness and made some coffee. She laughed about the experience and joked about feeding the fish. She said to be careful of the green fish when they went diving. They had anchored in 20 feet of water, and they were within 100 feet of the reef where they planned to dive. The plan would be to launch themselves off the swim platform at the back of the boat. They would use the buddy system they were all familiar with. Bev would buddy with Debbie, and John would buddy with Suzie. The plan would be to dive together as a group of four.

The Complication

John and Bev hauled out four scuba tanks from the starboard cockpit locker and laid them out on the cockpit floor. Each of them had a duffle bag of scuba gear and knew how to get ready. They strapped the backpacks onto the tanks and then the regulator. They connected the hoses to the buoyancy compensator, then turned the tanks on to make sure everything was working. Although the temperature of the ocean water was warm, they each donned 3mm wetsuits for protection from any jellyfish and sea anemones. The wrist computer would calculate their nitrogen absorption and let them know if they need a decompression stop. They planned to stop at 10 feet anyway for 2 minutes. The wrist computer also had a compass, depth gauge, and measured how much air they had left in the tank.

A briefing about hand signals and a dive plan discussion occurred before they moved the tanks to the swim platform and slipped their arms into the backpack straps. After spitting into the mask, they rubbed the glass to keep it from fogging while underwater. They slipped the fins onto each foot. They checked each other's tanks to make sure everything was in order, then one by one, they slipped into the water.

The first part of the dive was to snorkel 100 feet to the reef on the surface. Once they arrived over the top of the reef, they would signal to descend and meet in 30 feet of water before beginning to explore. John signaled to the group to begin the descent. It needed to be a slow descent, so John would have time to clear his ears. As a child, John ruptured his eardrums following an ear infection. He found that the increase in water pressure from descending deeper caused his ears to pain. Although the ear pressure would equalize, it took longer than the average scuba diver.

John was the last one of the four to reach the reef in 30 feet of water. He signaled to the group that he was OK and motioned to head along the reef. Brightly colored coral allowed the small sergeant fish to swim in and out as if to attack to protect their turf. This never failed to amuse John. These tiny 2 cm long fish thought they could scare him away by rushing at him from the depths of the coral.

John felt a tap on his shoulder. Suzie pointed to a puffer fish that had inflated itself. Bev pulled out his iPhone in the specially protected diving casing and, using a flash, took a picture. There were large grouper fish floating by, barely moving a muscle as they drifted past them on their way. Debbie pointed to something green under a rock, and a large moray eel poked out his head and bared its teeth. Bev took a picture of that as well.

They descended to 60 feet, and their dive plan had them there for 2 minutes. The rocks at that depth were barren of coral as it was too deep for the sunlight to penetrate. Sometimes at that depth, a shark would appear, but not today. The four of them signaled to each other to ascend back to 30 feet. John was the last one to leave and was about to ascend when something caught the corner of his eye. He turned around, and not 3 feet from him was another diver. John's first thought was perhaps there was something wrong with the diver, because there were no bubbles coming from the regulator. John stared at the man, who was struggling slightly to keep from going deeper by moving his arms. It was then that John realized he was holding a diving knife in his right hand.

There was no mistaking the piercing dark eyes of the man. It was Rick.

Chapter 23

Rick was lying in bed in Nonsuch Bay resort, Antigua. It had been a week since he agreed to the job. This was the way to live, he thought. The woman who visited him last night cost $200, a bargain. His ex-wife wanted half his salary, but the joke was on her because he had no salary to share with her. The $32,000 in bitcoin had already jumped to $50,000. That, along with the $18,000 in bitcoin for the first job which had increased to $30,000, gave him more money than he had ever seen in his life. He must have done a good job with the first one, because they wanted him to do the same to John Hegarty. It felt great to let John know he was going after him when he ran into him and his crew on the beach last night.

His job was to make John Hegarty's death look like an accident. The evening prior to coming to Antigua to do the job, he reviewed the instructions on the dark web page. The dark web page detailed the sailing trip information John was going to make, including the charter company. An invoice was part of the package on the website. This included an $800 rental for scuba tanks for the 10 days.

Although Rick would never claim to be the smartest person on the planet, he knew that scuba diving accidents happened frequently. It was the perfect accident. There would be no witnesses, and they could not identify him as the perpetrator, as the accident would happen under the water. The one obstacle Rick identified early on was he did not know how to scuba dive. DiveCarib in English Harbour offered beginner lessons. This was the first stop when he arrived. He offered to pay the instructor $2000 for two 8-hour days of instruction. The other demand was to learn on a rebreather.

The rebreather regulator allowed the air to be recirculated after it absorbed the CO_2 from the air. This would cause no bubbles, and a diver would be undetected from the surface where the bubbles would appear. This would be another layer to prevent Rick from detection when the accident occurred. Although Rick knew little about scuba diving, his excellent swimming skills developed from being sent to camp in Ontario during the summers. His father had no intention of looking after him when school was out for the summer holidays.

"You cannot learn about rebreathing scuba until you have mastered single tank diving," explained Jimmy, the PADI scuba diving instructor.

"Then, I'll find someone else to relieve me of the $2000," replied Rick. He was standing in front of the scuba dive shop. "You need to teach me the basics in the next 2 days, so I can go diving early next week." Rick made a few steps to walk away. If Jimmy wouldn't teach him, he'd find someone else. It was a competitive market and there were plenty of other dive shops on the island.

"Wait!" said Jimmy.

Jimmy looked around to be sure none of his diving instructors were around. This was an unusual request. If the dive school didn't teach by the protocols that had been developed, they could face trouble, as scuba diving was all about safety. $2000 was a lot of money as business had been slow of late. He quickly calculated that the usual rate for this kind of lesson was $750, so he could pocket the rest of the money.

"Ok, but if anyone asks, tell them you have been diving for years and want to learn how you can stay underwater longer by using the rebreather," said Jimmy. "That way, there won't be questions."

"Let's get started then," said Rick.

Jimmy and Rick spent the morning in the classroom. The course outline was to understand the basics of how the pressure of the water increases as you dive deeper, causing more nitrogen to be dissolved in the bloodstream and tissues.

"If too much nitrogen accumulated under the water," said Jimmy, "it would cause nitrogen bubbles to develop in the joints and blood vessels. The joint pain from the bubbles caused 'the bends' as the diver would bend to create more space in the joint to relieve the pain. The bubbles of nitrogen in the blood would cause strokes as they plugged the cerebral vessels and paralysis as the bubbles plugged the blood vessels into the spinal cord. To prevent this, the modern dive computers would calculate the nitrogen accumulation and alert the diver to do a decompression stop."

Rick yawned and thought to himself, this reminds me too much of high school. I need to get out of here.

"If you ascend too quickly, you must remember to breathe out to prevent the lungs from bursting as the air expands," explained Jimmy. "If you were doing a single tank dive, you would ascend at the same rate as the bubbles. With the rebreather, you could lose perspective as there would be no bubbles to follow, and you might ascend too quickly."

Rick sighed and looked at his watch. "Can we get on with the diving part of the program?" asked Rick.

They spent a few hours in the pool in the afternoon. Jimmy took Rick to the end of the dock, and Rick had his first dive in the ocean. It was a lot easier than he had expected. He felt like a natural under the water and thought the rebreather was easy to use. The session lasted an hour, and Rick learned how to use the buoyancy compensator to control his depth.

The following day, Jimmy took Rick to a nearby reef. They spent most of the time at 30 feet, but Jimmy took him to a depth of 60 feet late in the afternoon. They practiced a decompression stop at 10 feet. When Jimmy signaled Rick to the surface, they came to the surface near the dive boat. "You are a fast learner!" said Jimmy. "As of now, you are a certified diver. Congratulations! You can have the equipment, including a full tank, for one day next week."

After Jimmy drove the dive boat back to the dock at English Harbour, Rick hopped into a taxi and instructed the driver to take him to Jolly Harbour. He knew John was not arriving until the late evening. Rick knew the sailboat's name to be Happy Days 1 from the documents he had received on the dark web. With him, he had several simple GPS trackers. This was the same technology used for tracking lost luggage, but these were waterproof. Walking onto the dock, he found the sailboat named Happy Days 1. He strategically positioned the two GPS trackers to avoid detection, one on the mast, the other in the dinghy.

The following day, he saw on his cellphone that the boat had not moved, so he hopped in a taxi to Jolly Harbour. Walking to the other side of the marina, he saw a red cigarette boat. He hopped into the driver's seat and pulled out his binoculars. He was watching the two gorgeous bikini-clad women on the foredeck of Happy Days 1 when John walked up to them. For some reason, John looked up directly at him. Rick found it amusing that John had spotted him. He thought it even more amusing when he saw the fear on his face when he turned his hand into a gun and pretended to pull the trigger.

Rick tracked the sailboat to English Harbour and then to Green Island. This was a well-known spot for divers, and Rick was ready to dive. He had rented a small Boston Whaler and arrived in Rickett Harbor on the other side of Green Island shortly after them. Green Island blocked their view of his small launch so they couldn't see him. Keeping just out of their view, he watched them through his binoculars, get their diving gear together and then slip into the water. He motored to the west of the reef and threw the anchor. The water had a visibility of 30 feet, and he could see where they were by following their bubbles on the surface. After donning his scuba tank, mask, fins and snorkel, he launched himself into the water. He was following them using his snorkel. Rick had the rebreather ready for the dive. He could not see them through the water, so Rick was certain they could not see him on the surface. It was easy to follow their bubbles. The map on his computer showed the depths at 60 feet. Rick knew it was time to make his move. Deflating the buoyancy compensator, he rapidly descended to 60 feet.

As luck would have it, he leveled at 60 feet behind a large boulder. Peering from the boulder, he saw John was the closest to him. The others appeared to move up the sloping sea floor to the shallow reef. Rick swam out from the rock just as John turned to face him. The fear in his eyes confirmed Rick had the advantage of surprise.

Rick grabbed John's air hose from the tank to the regulator and sliced it open. The air from John's tank escaped in a torrent, as Rick felt the satisfaction of, yet another job well done.

Chapter 24

John watched in disbelief as the severed air hose waved madly in the water. He knew the air would run out completely in about 2 minutes, leaving him with an empty tank. He spat out his severed regulator and watched it sink to the bottom of the rocks. John reached around, grabbed his auxiliary octopus regulator, and placed it in his mouth. Rick had cut the air hose close to where it joined the regulator, leaving about three feet of hose still attached to the tank. John grabbed the end of the hose as it flew past his field of vision. Tying a knot into the loose hose took him 10 seconds to stop the air leak.

John watched Rick's smug expression through his mask turn to shock as John approached him. Rick reached down to grab his sheathed knife, now strapped to his left inner calf. John grabbed Rick's mask and tore it from his face. The mask drifted to the bottom. Now, Rick could no longer see. With his other hand, John pulled the regulator from Rick's mouth. Rick's hands were flailing madly, trying to find a part of John he could attack. John placed his fin against Rick's chest while he pulled with all his might on the regulator and hose. The regulator separated from the hose, and air leaked, making the regulator useless. If Rick tried to use it, he would get a lungful of water.

The Complication

John watched as Rick's panic set in. Backing away from Rick so he was now 10 feet away, he saw Rick pull the emergency valve of the buoyancy regulator. At first, nothing seemed to happen. John noticed the bladder of the compensatory fill up with air. Within seconds, Rick started the ascent towards the surface. He seemed to accelerate rapidly as he ascended out of view. John slowly followed him to the surface. Following the bubbles as he rose, John easily controlled his ascent.

Rick could feel panic as he pulled the emergency cord of his buoyancy regulator. He needed air, and he needed air now. The urge to take a deep breath was overwhelming. Rick knew he was rising quickly as he passed the bubbles leaking from his regulator as he rose to the surface. He felt tight in his chest and resisted the temptation to breathe out and take in a lungful of water. Suddenly, he felt a terrible pain in his chest. He was a 30-pack-year smoker, and his doctor told him there were blebs of damaged lung at the apex of each lung. The doctor told him they could pop anytime, and he needed to stop smoking. In that fleeting moment, he wished he had listened to his doctor. When he arrived at the surface, he tried to breathe deeply, but nothing happened. He tried again before he blacked out.

Dive medicine fascinated John when he was in medical school, and he trained to be certified in running the hyperbaric chamber. He had studied many of the injuries from diving-related accidents. John suspected that with Rick's rate of ascent, his lungs had probably ruptured. The pressure at 60 feet was three times that of the surface. If Rick had held his breath on the way up, the air in his lungs would expand 3 times, causing inevitable lung rupture. John had seen no one with a ruptured lung from diving, but he had observed that in the ICU, sometimes even a slight increase in ventilator pressure could cause lung rupture. To manage this and decompress the pneumothorax, doctors would insert a chest tube between the lung and chest wall and hook the tube to an underwater seal. This would allow the trapped air to leak out but not allow the air to leak back in.

By the time John got to the surface, Rick was unconscious. He removed his mask and placed it on his forehead. Cautiously, he approached Rick. The buoyancy compensatory was so distended it was rock hard, and Rick's body was nearly halfway out of the water, floating horizontally. John felt for a pulse. It was weak. He palpated the neck and noticed immediately that Rick's trachea was pushed to the right side of his neck. John had only seen this in the emergency room in patients with tension pneumothorax. Severely elevated pressure inside the chest caused the trachea to be pushed to the other side of the neck. The compression of the superior vena cava, the major vessel returning blood to the heart, would lead to cardiac arrest if they did not treat the tension pneumothorax promptly.

The Complication

John grabbed the collar of Rick's wetsuit and dragged him to the swim platform of the sailboat. Bev, Debbie and Suzie, sensing a problem, had ascended to the surface. Bev and John hauled Rick out of the water and laid him on the swim platform. He still had a weak pulse but was not breathing. John instructed Suzie to bring him his doctor's bag while Bev cut the wetsuit from Rick's body. John opened his doctor's bag and retrieved a plastic-handled scalpel. He plunged it into Rick's left chest, and a sudden gush of air escaped. John pushed his finger into the hole to make the defect larger, and another huge gush of air came out. Rick took an involuntary gasp of air, although he was still unconscious.

John did not have a chest tube in his doctor's bag but had a Foley catheter. They normally used the Foley catheter to drain urine from the bladder, but because it was a large one, John pushed it into the hole in the chest and sutured it in place. A balloon was at the end, so he blew this up with 10 cc of saline solution to prevent it from dislodging. Every breath resulted in air escaping out of the open end of the Foley catheter. Rick was moving by now, so they dragged him into the cockpit. He was getting quite restless and seemed to be confused. Suzie ran into the main salon and retrieved zip ties. They tied his hand behind his back and zip-tied his legs together. They zip-tied both the arms and legs to the cockpit table so he wouldn't fall overboard.

John went to the VHF radio and turned it on to Channel 16, the emergency channel. He held the mouthpiece and said, "Mayday, Mayday, Mayday, this is sailing vessel Happy Days 1, Happy Days 1, Happy Days 1. There has been a diving accident on Green Island. We need a boat to take an injured man to the hospital. He has a pneumothorax and is unconscious but breathing."

There was no answer in 30 seconds, so John repeated the message. This time, there was a response. "Sailing vessel Happy Days 1, Happy Days 1, Happy Days 1, this Antigua Search and Rescue. Go to Channel 71."

John switched channels, told the Search and Rescue team about the injury, and that he inserted a chest tube. They responded by saying they were 20 minutes away.

When the Search and Rescue team arrived, Rick was awake and combative. Fortunately, John and Bev had him adequately restrained by the zip ties, so he could not jump into the water. It was difficult to know whether this was because Rick was confused or whether he was normally combative when he lost control. The Search and Rescue team loaded him on a carrying board and strapped him down on a bench at the stern of their boat. As they were lifting him, he almost slid into the water, but the four burly Antiguans carrying the board controlled the struggling Rick by brute force. The team said they would send someone to make a report later.

John, Debbie, Bev, and Suzie spent the next hour getting the dive gear put away. They lowered the dinghy so Suzie and Debbie could search for Rick's gear, which they found floating in the harbor near the beach on the north side of Green Island after an hour. They piled everything onto the cockpit floor, thinking the police might want to look at it. As they sat around the table in the main salon, Bev said, "I think we all need a drink."

Bev pulled out a bottle of overproof rum and poured each of them a thimbleful. "Here's to a boring and uneventful rest of the trip," he said as they clinked glasses and knocked back the poisonous liquid.

Suzie made a face as she headed to the fridge. "I'll stick to my white wine." She poured herself a large glass and opened 3 bottles of beer for the others. They quietly sipped their drinks, letting the day's events sink in.

"We need to talk about what happened," said John. "It will help us sort out the events and if there is anything else we need to do now."

They talked for the next 2 hours about what happened. John repeated the story of his encounter with Rick in 60 feet of water. The rest of the group marveled at his quick thinking and lightning action. They talked about medical emergencies while diving and how to prevent them. John could not say why Rick wanted to harm him. He could have just as easily knifed him on the beach the other night, and nobody would have seen it. They discussed canceling the rest of the trip in favor of going back to Toronto. No one wanted to do that, preferring to stay in the tropical paradise for the remaining time.

When they heard the noise of a speed boat approaching, they stopped talking and went up to the cockpit. The blue flashing lights announced the arrival of the police as they pulled up alongside the sailboat.

"Are you okay if we come aboard?" asked the driver of the police boat.

"Of course," said John. "We'll tie you up at the stern so you can come up to the swim platform."

There were three police officers on the speedboat. The leader introduced himself as Jack. His age was 30, and he had a shaved head. There was a wide smile with bright white teeth surrounded by a well-trimmed goatee beard. He boarded the sailboat from the swim platform. The other 2 police officers remained on the speedboat.

Jack declined the offer of coffee or water to drink. "Perhaps you could tell me what happened?" asked Jack.

John recounted the story of the diving accident. He described Rick as having some kind of personal vendetta against him. John told him about the death of Joe Sawchuk and the pathologist Derek.

John explained that there must be a link between these events, but he was struggling to find it.

"Rick is telling a different story," said Jack. "He says you are the one who attacked him under the water, almost killing him. You shoved a tube in his chest, trying to finish the job you had started but failed. The only thing that saved him was the others who restrained you."

Bev pulled up the video feeds on his laptop. The video images from the cockpit and the stern of the boat were clear. The time stamps showed everything that occurred was as John described. Jack smiled at the videos. "I don't see any cameras in the cockpit or anywhere else. Are we being videotaped now?" He asked.

Bev explained the cameras were tiny, and he fixed the solar panels to the top of the bimini. The video feeds were to record any encounter with Rick. They were all worried he would try something and wanted to be alerted if he came on board.

"I would suggest you speak with Sidney Noseworthy, the police detective who knows what happened in Toronto," John said. "I'll get his contact information." John went down to his cabin and retrieved the information from his wallet. He wrote the phone number on a piece of paper, along with his phone number, and gave it to Jack.

"Thanks for speaking with me," said Jack. "I'll be in touch with you." Jack walked to the swim platform and untied the line to the police boat. He hopped on board and started the engine. He reversed away from the sailboat before putting it forward and pushing the throttle lever forward to the maximum.

The four on the sailboat watched as the police boat sped away. Suzie spoke first, saying, "Do you think they will arrest Rick?"

"I certainly hope so," said John. "I would like to discover the true story behind what is happening."

Debbie and Suzie offered to make fettuccini and sausages for dinner. While they prepared the dinner, Bev and John sat in the cockpit. The sun was going down, but Green Island blocked the view of the sunset. The skies, however, lit up to magnificent colors of red and orange in the fading daylight. Within 15 minutes, the skies went black, and the stars appeared. "What if there are more than Rick after me?" asked John.

"Although anything is possible, I think it is unlikely," replied Bev. "Rick is the only one we have seen. He was alone when he threatened you in Toronto, and we have seen only him on this trip. There does not appear to be anyone else."

"Do you think I am putting the rest of you at risk?" asked John. "I seem to be the target. Maybe continuing the trip is not the best idea."

"You have disabled the culprit," answered Bev. "We have no evidence there is anyone else after you. When we talked about it this afternoon, the girls were quite adamant. They want to continue the trip. I say we carry on."

John was about to say something when his phone went off. It was a 268 number, indicating it was from Antigua. John answered the phone.

"This is Jack. We spoke on your boat earlier this afternoon. Rick has escaped from the hospital," said Jack. "We went to arrest him after speaking with Sidney Noseworthy. His hospital bed was empty. He was gone, along with all the chest tube gear."

Chapter 25

Ainslie was looking at the short video. The image was clear, and she could see the faces of the couple who walked into the apartment. The man was tall, perhaps 6'2". He was slightly balding, and she guessed his age to be about 50. The woman was shorter and oriental. Ainslie could not guess her age but was younger than the man. They were walking side by side until they got to the door of apartment 2401. The man reached into his pocket and pulled out the keys. He opened the door. They both walked into the apartment and closed the door.

Ainslie was good with computers, but not as good as her friend Adrian. He was a year older than Ainslie at 13 and worked at Best Buy on the Geek Squad team after school. His job was to load new computers with the programs the buyers had ordered. Sometimes, clients would bring in older, slow computers, and he would remove all the viruses, worms and other illicit programs that made their way onto the hard drive. When things were slow, he and his other Geek Squad colleagues scoured the dark web for interesting information.

He was at Best Buy on the dark web when Ainslie called him. He had finished loading the programs on the computer that a client was picking up later that evening and had some time. No other jobs were pending. Browsing the dark web was one of his favorite fringe benefits of working there.

"Hey," she said to Adrian.

"Hey," he replied.

"My dad had his identity stolen," explained Ainslie. "All his emails and passwords are on the dark web. Someone bought $32,000 worth of bitcoin using his American Express card. I called him to change all his passwords and other information."

"Wow," said Adrian. "That sucks!"

Ainslie told him about finding her dad's name on a random web page. She mentioned she thought something was happening, but her dad was not digitally smart enough to figure it out. She asked if he could check out a few things for her. Adrian became quite animated with the digital sleuthing proposition.

"That sounds like fun!" he said. "I'll get right on it. I have time now, but it may take me a day or two."

The following night, Adrian called Ainslie. "Very interesting. I found a few things. There are often trails on the dark web. Sometimes if the encryption gets too complicated, it might take a while, but usually, I can find something. They made the Bitcoin purchase on a MacBook Pro laptop from an apartment on Lakeshore

Boulevard, apartment 2401. A numbered company owns the apartment. I have been unsuccessful at tracing the company number to a name.

"I looked for the website you mentioned, but someone had removed it. I played around with the numbers and letters on the web address you gave me and came across some sites similar to what you described. A lady was holding a piece of paper. When I clicked on the paper, there was a menu of services. They were all written in Mandarin. Google translated the Mandarin into English for me. Maybe something got lost in the translation, but the choices were wild. They included accidental death, broken legs, removal of one eye, and a few other crazy options.

"Ainslie, I think someone wants to hurt your dad," concluded Adrian.

Ainslie was quiet on the other end of the phone before she spoke. "I thought something like that was going on. Do you think the Bitcoin purchase was a payment of sorts?"

"The beauty of Bitcoin is that it is untraceable," said Adrian. "The events must be related because both the website and the identity theft occurred around the same time."

"How do I find out who lives in apartment 2401?" asked Ainslie.

"I have a few ideas," said Adrian. "Do you have some free time tomorrow? I'm not working."

They met at the subway station. Adrian was carrying a black backpack over his right shoulder. He had a peach fuzz growth of hair over his chin, upper lip and face. He wore thick glasses with large black frames. His pants were two inches too short, and the socks he was wearing had unique patterns from each other and were different colors. His white running shoes were grey, and the untied shoelaces dragged on the ground. He had no jacket but wore a long-sleeved sweater with a V-neck.

"There is no way we will get caught," said Adrian. "The toughest part is getting in through the front door. We can wait until someone enters with an UberEATS. Then we can follow them inside and up the elevators to the penthouses."

It took them 20 minutes on the subway to get to the closest subway stop to the apartment. They walked another 15 minutes to get to Lakeshore Boulevard. It was December in Toronto, and the wind blew off the lake with a cold, blustery bite. There was a sprinkling of snow getting blown around by the wind. It was minus 5 degrees Celsius. Neither Ainslie nor Adrian seemed to be bothered by the nasty winter weather.

The entrance lobby was well-lit, and a security camera focused on the entry keypad. Ainslie and Adrian waited outside the lobby between the double doors to escape the wind. It did not take long for an UberEATS driver to walk up to the door and call the person who ordered the food to let him in. Ainslie and Adrian scooted in behind him before the door closed. There were security videos in the elevator lobby and the elevator. They took the elevator to the 24th floor, the penthouse floor. There were no security cameras in the hallway.

Adrian set his backpack on the carpeted floor and removed some equipment. He pulled out three small devices. "These tiny cameras have motion detection," he explained to Ainslie, "so the batteries will last about one or two weeks. A client returned them to the store and got a refund. The devices were a little scratched, so the boss discarded them. I always go through the garbage looking for this kind of stuff. I have a drawer full of junk like this at home. They will use the Wi-Fi from 2401 and broadcast to your and my cellphone."

Suite 2401 was at the end of the hall. There was an exit sign just before the entrance of the suite. Adrian applied 2 sided sticky pads to tiny cameras. Ainslie climbed onto his shoulders and placed the 3 cameras so they were aiming down the hallway. They checked their cell phones. The cameras were in a suitable position. They could see who came out of the elevators and who entered suite 2401.

Ainslie hopped off Adrian's shoulders. They gave each other a high-five and went to the elevators, the main lobby, and out the door. Walking back to the subway station was less cold because the wind was at their backs. Adrian lived close to a different stop and got off first to go home. Ainslie arrived at her stop and walked the three blocks to her home.

Ainslie synced her phone with her computer and logged onto the video. There was already a video waiting for her to watch. After looking at the two walking down the hallway and into suite 2401, she thought about how she could find their names. One possibility was to go through their mail. She discarded that because the mailboxes did not correspond to the suite number. There would be no way to go through their garbage. Maybe Adrian could hack into their email? That might be too much to ask. He had already done enough. The easiest way would be to send the video to her dad to see if he recognized them.

John picked up on the first ring. "Hi Honey. Is everything okay?"

"Hi, dad," she responded. "I sent you a video to your email. Do you recognize the two people?"

"Just a minute, honey," said John. "I'll open up my computer." John went from the cockpit to the main salon, where he sat with the others. They had just finished the fettuccini and sausages. John opened the computer and logged into his email. John downloaded the video attachment and clicked on 'play'. He immediately recognized Nigel, his chief of staff, and his girlfriend, Rebecca. He had met Rebecca at several hospital functions but never spoke with her.

"That's a video of Nigel, my chief of staff, and his girlfriend, Rebecca, walking down a hallway," said John. "Why are you showing me this?"

Ainslie went quiet. She wasn't sure how much she should tell him. She didn't want to get Adrian in trouble. Ainslie knew her dad would be mad at her for invading someone's privacy. His chief of staff of all people. She was at a loss for words. Maybe she should just hang up?

"Ainslie," said John, "are you still there?"

A thought crossed Ainslie's mind. Her dad was always preaching to her about honesty and telling the truth. "Dad," she said, "you need to tell me what is happening. You always tell me to be honest, yet you have not been honest with me. If you tell me what is happening, I'll tell you about the video. If not, I am hanging up right now."

John sighed, "Honey, you are 12 years old. I can't burden you with problems that are going on in my life. It might cause you anxiety. At your age, you need to focus on yourself."

"Dad," Ainslie said, "That's a load of crap. Either you tell me everything or this conversation is over!"

John had always had a great relationship with Ainslie. She trusted him and admired him. This conversation put him at a crossroads. She was asking him to trust her. Why did she have to grow up so quickly? Ainslie knew things were happening, and John now believed she would eventually find out.

"Okay, honey," said John, "You asked for it!" John told Ainslie the story, beginning with the surgical complication following the gallbladder operation performed by Joe Sawchuk and ending with the scuba diving accident. It took about an hour. Ainslie told John everything she had been up to, including Adrian's findings on the dark web. She told him that there was no doubt someone was out to kill him, and Nigel was involved.

"What will you do now, Dad?" she asked.

"I need to think about everything and talk with my crew members," said John. "Do you think your friend Adrian would talk with the police if you asked him?"

"I suspect he would do anything I asked," said Ainslie. "I think he likes me."

Yikes, thought John. He had no idea how to respond to that comment. Instead, he said, "Let me call you tomorrow. Ainslie, thanks for telling me what you know."

"Thanks for trusting me," she replied. They hung up the phone.

While John was on the phone with Ainslie, the others cleaned up the dishes and the cockpit table. They were waiting for him in the cockpit when he sat down. John told him what Ainslie had been up to and how it might affect them. "If they have paid someone to kill me, and we have now disabled him, do you think they will send someone else?"

"I doubt that will happen," said Bev. "It is too risky. Besides, it sounds like Rick is on the loose again. I would vote to move on to Great Bird Island and hide out there." Bev pulled out his cell phone and showed everyone on the map where it was. "It's about a 2-hour sail away from here, and the only way to get there is by boat. We will rig the electric current through the lifelines every night, and we will remain vigilant. I doubt he will find us."

The rest of the group agreed.

"We'll leave first thing in the morning," said John.

Chapter 26

The view from the top of Great Bird Island was memorable. Their sailboat looked tiny in the bay, gently moving in the small waves of the protected harbor. There was only one other sailboat in the anchorage, although John expected more sailboats would arrive throughout the day. They anchored Happy Days 1 in 15 feet of clear blue water. There were colorful reefs, and they had already spotted large rays as they gracefully glided past the sailboat after they had anchored. They took the dinghy to the closest beach and found the trail to take them to the summit.

They could see the town of Parnham two kilometers away. Many birds were flying in the open skies above the island. The largest seagulls John had ever seen were flying overhead. It was a protected habitat and attracted pelicans and many other bird species. They had spotted a harmless snake, the Antiguan Racer snake, but took a wide berth so they would not frighten the snake. The deserted beaches had champagne-colored sand. This was the paradise that they had been searching for.

After taking many pictures, they returned to the beach. They loaded themselves into the dinghy and motored to the sailboat. Bev and John finished making the sandwiches for lunch and brought them to the cockpit. Suzie had poured herself a large glass of wine, and the others were drinking beer.

The Complication

"This is truly paradise," sighed Suzie. "A toast to great friends, grand adventure, and conquering adversity together!" They clinked their glasses and beer bottles together and had a long drink.

"Who's up for snorkeling?" asked Debbie. They all hooted in agreement. They each wore wetsuits, masks, and fins before sliding into the warm Caribbean water. The reef was less than 50 feet from their boat and was in 10 to 15 feet of water. They could see colorful corral and many small fish. Overfishing around Antigua resulted in a scarcity of large fish in the reefs, but there were large rays and massive lobsters that tucked themselves away in the shelter of large rocks. Only their antennae peeked out from their hiding places. There were colorful jellyfish and small crabs that scooted around the rocks of the reef. Bev took a picture of a massive turtle that swam within 5 feet of them. After an hour, they headed back to the sailboat.

Sitting in the cockpit under the protection of the bimini, they all agreed that it was the best snorkeling they had ever experienced. They agreed to spend at least 3 days in this tropical paradise of Great Bird Island before they continued their circumnavigation trip around Antigua. They spent the rest of the afternoon reading and playing backgammon. John spent the afternoon on the laptop, looking at the dark web. Adrian had taken pictures of the websites he had discovered, but someone had already removed some. John found the same thing as Adrian from the ones that were still active. There was a list of menus where one could choose accident, dismemberment, eye removal, and other services.

John shook his head. There was more going on than just someone coming after him. He needed to find out more about Nigel. When he did a Google search, he discovered they had selected him as the next Deputy Minister of Health. He was to start in a month. He tried to search for Rebecca but did not know her last name. A thought crossed his mind. He needed to speak with Ainslie. It was 5 PM, so she would be home from school. She answered on the first ring.

"Hi honey," he said, "I wanted to ask you a favor. Could Adrian determine whether that computer in 2401 accessed those websites on the dark web? I don't know enough about these things to know whether that is possible."

"No problem, dad," said Ainslie. "I'll ask him. Is everything all right? I don't like that Rick is running around. He should be in jail."

"Don't worry," said John. "I severely disabled him, and he has a chest tube hanging out of his chest. Besides, there is no way he can find us in this remote location."

"Dad," said Ainslie, "what if he placed a luggage tracker somewhere on your boat? Maybe check around for that?"

"You are getting more paranoid than me," laughed John. "This fellow is not the sharpest tool in the shed. There is no way he could think of something like that."

They said their goodbyes and promised to speak to each other tomorrow. John sat with Bev and Debbie, who were playing backgammon. He told them that Adrian would see if there was a connection between the laptop from 2401 and the disturbing dark web pages. He half-heartedly mentioned Ainslie's suggestion to look for luggage tracking devices on board.

Bev bolted upright. "She's right!" Bev cried out. "I have been trying to understand how he knew where we were. There is no way it was a lucky guess. There must be a device on board. Debbie and Suzie, you two look inside the boat. Check all the cupboards and behind the corners. John and I will check outside.

It took John and Bev only 10 minutes to find the tracker attached to the mast. He called Debbie and Suzie. They came running up to the deck of the sailboat. It was a round object about the size of a Canadian toonie, but twice as thick. Bev placed it on the deck and crushed it with his foot. He picked up the damaged tracker and threw it overboard.

"When they carted him away on the rescue boat, he did not have his cellphone or anything else," reflected John. "I think we are safe that he does not know where we are, but as much as we like this place, we should change locations tomorrow. Maybe we can go to Deep Bay. There is supposed to be great diving there, and we still have 4 full tanks as part of the rental package."

"We cannot be too careful," replied Bev. John nodded in agreement.

They baked Mahi Mahi in the oven that evening. There was fresh garlic bread, green beans and rice. It was a group preparation, and they each had an assignment. Suzie prepared the fish using garlic, onions, fresh tomatoes cut into small cubes and some potion that she said was a secret. John prepared the garlic bread, Debbie cooked the green beans, and Bev prepared the rice in the cooker. They agreed it was one of the best dinners of the trip.

After dinner, they sat in the cockpit and talked for a while. Debbie and Bev said they were calling it an early night. They were tired after all the day's activities and were ready to pass out. Suzie and John climbed onto the foredeck to stargaze. They lay on cushions, with John partially leaning against the mast and Suzie leaning her head against John's abdomen. "Look," said Suzie, "there's Orion's belt! I can't believe how bright the stars are out here." She pointed out the Big Dipper, the Little Dipper and the North Star.

"Despite the problems we've had," she said, "this has been the best trip of my life. This is everything I have ever dreamed paradise would be like." She sighed. "The best part for me is being here with you. I feel safe. I wish you and me could stay here forever."

Suzie sat up. There were tears in her eyes. "John, I am so happy. Thank you for bringing me." She touched his face and leaned forward to kiss him. John closed his eyes. He was unsure he was ready for this but felt powerless to resist. For the past few days, he knew he was developing feelings for her. John felt comfortable in her company. He found her exceptionally attractive; best of all, she looked at him like he was the most desirable man on earth. The power of her reciprocal attraction flooded his senses. For John, that created an irresistible force from which he was powerless to resist. He knew there was nothing he could do to stop what was about to happen.

A loud crash that came from the foredeck, followed by a burst of flames, interrupted the moment.

Chapter 27

The fire rapidly spread on the foredeck. John and Suzie jumped from their resting position against the mast and shouted to Bev and Debbie to bring the fire extinguisher. Suzie raced into the main salon to search for fire extinguishers. There was one in each of the cabins near the entrance door. John raced to the galley and retrieved the fire blanket. He threw it over the fire, but the blanket only covered part of the fire. The fire continued to burn around the edges of the fire blanket.

Upon hearing the commotion, Bev woke up from his slumbers and ran from his forward cabin to the main salon. He grabbed the fire extinguisher near the stove. It was the largest one on the boat and looked brand new. He unclipped it and, holding it by the nozzle, bolted up the companionway and to the foredeck.

Bev pulled the pin on the fire extinguisher and covered the remaining flames with the contents of the cylinder. This put the fire out. However, as John lifted the fire blanket, the flames reignited. Bev covered the flames with the white fluid from the fire extinguisher. This took care of the blaze. A few embers fizzled out within a few seconds in the thick white liquid. John and Bev were both out of breath as they stared at the damage.

The blaze had blackened and buckled the foredeck. Broken glass from a bottle was on the deck. The impact shattered the glass into small pieces, but there were a few larger pieces with some writing, 'Baca'. John suspected this was part of a bottle of Bacardi rum. John looked around at the water surrounding them but saw nothing.

"Bev, can you get the spotlight and binoculars?" asked John. "We need to find out who threw this at us. Bring the bag of flares. We need to alert anyone that we need help. It might scare the perpetrator away."

Bev came back with the spotlight and shined it around the boat. About one hundred feet away was a Boston Whaler. Although it was dark, the spotlight lit up the boat. John could see a lone figure at the stern of the boat. Looking through the binoculars, there was no doubt it was Rick. His size gave him away. He was pouring liquid from a red plastic gasoline container into a bottle. John saw him stuff a rag into the end of the bottle. Rick walked up to the helm of the Boston Whaler, carrying the bottle of gasoline in one hand and a square plastic box, which John recognized as the underwater seal for the chest tube to keep the lung expanded. They heard the engines roar as he aimed the bow of the boat at them, stopping 10 feet from the sailboat's stern. He lit the rag at the end of the bottle and lobbed it into the cockpit, where it smashed on impact. The explosion caused an enormous flame. The impact knocked John and Bev off the boat's deck and against the lifelines. They watched as their fire extinguisher rolled into the ocean.

Debbie and Suzie were in the main salon, each with a fire extinguisher. They pulled the safety pin and squeezed the handle. Through the open companionway, they soaked the cockpit with the liquid. The bimini and dodger had caught fire. Spraying the fire extinguisher from below did nothing to retard the flames that enveloped the canvas structures. Both extinguishers were empty. There was only one fire extinguisher left, but the blaze from the canvas was out of control.

"We better get ready to abandon the boat," cried Suzie. "Grab your and Bev's passports, wallets and phones, and I'll grab mine. John left his on the captain's table with his wallet and cell phone. I'll grab those."

Bev saw the fire spread quickly to the bimini and dodger. The fire trapped the two women inside the boat, soon to be turned into an inferno. He opened the forward hatch at the front of the boat and jumped into the forward cabin. He needed to ensure Suzie and Debbie were all right and get them safely. The bimini and dodger were burning out of control, and it would only be a matter of minutes before the entire boat caught fire. He ran into Debbie as he was rushing out of the door.

"We need to abandon the boat!" she screamed. Bev nodded in agreement.

"We attach the dinghy to the stern of the boat," said Bev. "Let's run under the dodger and bimini and hop on board before the boat catches fire. We'll pick John up on the bow."

Debbie grabbed the passports, wallets, and phones and shoved them in her pajama pockets. She followed Bev out of the companionway and onto the swim platform, ducking to avoid the cinders from the burning canvas. Suzie was right behind them. Once they boarded the dinghy, Suzie cut the line that attached them to the sailboat. They drifted away from the stern. Thick black smoke billowed from the sailboat, indicating the fiberglass was catching fire.

John, still on the foredeck, opened the bag of flares. There were several types. John opened the one that resembled a plastic gun and loaded it with what looked like a shotgun cartridge. The Boston Whaler was now on the starboard side of the sailboat twenty feet away. They designed these flares to fly two hundred feet in the sky. They were powerful. John aimed for the stern of the boat, where he had seen the plastic gas container, and fired. A bright orange flare lit up the ocean and hit the seat in the stern of the Boston Whaler with a loud thud. Nothing happened.

The explosion John was hoping for did not occur. He loaded another flare and aimed it at the Boston Whaler, which had now drifted to thirty feet from the sailboat. John could see Rick at the stern of the boat and aimed the flare towards him. Before he could launch the flare, there was a bright flash. He saw Rick's body launched ten feet into the air. A loud explosion followed this. Before John could brace himself, a giant blast of air threw him over the side of the boat and into the water.

John was treading water as he watched the fire on the sailboat spread rapidly. They made most modern sailboats of fiberglass, including Happy Days 1. Once a fire starts, the fiberglass is extremely flammable. This had cost sailors' lives more than once when their boat caught fire.

John panicked as he thought about Suzie, Debbie, and Bev. He swam as fast as he could towards the stern of the burning sailboat. The only thought on his mind was that he had to save them. This was all his fault. He could feel his heart race and his breathing increase as he swam. He could feel his torrent of tears getting washed away as he thrashed his arms wildly into the water, trying to get to the sailboat as quickly as possible.

"John!" yelled a voice in the darkness, "over here!" John stopped swimming and turned around. It was Suzie. She was standing at the front of the dinghy, waving her hands. John swam over to the dinghy and pulled himself on board. He was out of breath and could not speak. Suzie leaned down to him and asked, "Are you okay?" All John could do was nod in agreement. Debbie and Bev were at the rear of the dinghy.

"Let's get the fuck out of here!" said Bev as he revved the 10 hp engine to full throttle and headed for the town 2 kilometers away. John could talk now but had to shout over the roar of the outboard engine. Rick pulled back the throttle to reduce the noise from the engine so he could hear John.

"Wait!" cried John. "Let's check to see if there is anything left of Rick."

"That's crazy," said Bev. "He is on his own now. He tried to kill all of us."

"I saw him getting thrown in the air by the explosion," said John. "Let's make one circle around the burning Boston Whaler."

Reluctantly, Bev turned the dinghy back to the two burning vessels. He reduced the throttle and slowly approached the burning Boston Whaler. It was already sinking and listed to starboard at an alarming angle. Amongst other charred debris, there were floating charred cushions and lifejackets. Suzie retrieved the flashlight and swung the beam in a circle. There was a thud as the bow of the dinghy hit something. Suzie leaned over and focused the light on the object. She let out a bloodcurdling scream. "It's an arm!" she cried out.

They could see that the rest of Rick was in pieces a little further along. The explosions had attracted the sharks, and they were in a feeding frenzy. Boiling water around them from the sharks caused water to splash into the dinghy. The sharks were bumping into the hull of the dinghy with such force that the small boat was moving to the left and then to the right. The flashlight showed a sea of red.

This was close to where the explosion a few moments earlier had thrown John. The fiery inferno engulfed the entire sailboat, sending flames 50 feet into the sky. John and the others watched, mesmerized by the burning sailboat. The reflection on the water was bright orange. They stared at the burning boat as it listed to starboard and sank. The stern of the boat was the first part to sink. In slow motion, the rest of the hull went under the water over the next minute, and the flames went out. All that was sticking out of the water into the black sky was the mast as the remains of the sailboat settled in fifteen feet of water.

Bev put the engine in reverse and slowly backed away from the bloodbath and wreckage. Once clear of the destruction, he put the throttle in full forward and headed to the nearby village.

Chapter 28

"That's quite the story," said Sidney Noseworthy. He was sitting with John in the small interrogation room at the precinct in downtown Toronto. "Are you okay if we stop the recording?"

"Sure," replied John. "What do you think we should do next?"

Sidney pulled on his goatee and looked around the empty room. There was a notepad before him from when he made notes as John was talking. He was on the sixth page when John finished the story of everything that had happened on his trip south. The small recorder was next to the notepad. He got up from the chair and said to John. "We have been at this for 2 hours. I'll get some coffee and see how the others are doing. You take yours black, right?"

John nodded. The others had volunteered to come with John to the precinct. They split the four into separate rooms to see how closely their stories matched. John suspected that if the stories were identical in all aspects, the detective would conclude they contrived it. John was having difficulties believing everything that had happened. Bev suggested to the group that they not discuss the events until after they spoke to the police in Toronto. Their slight variation in recounting the events would add credibility to the story.

John thought back to that fateful night in Antigua. It took less than ten minutes in their dinghy to arrive at Parnham, the closest small town. They searched on the internet and discovered there was a police station. After googling, they found directions on Google Maps. They had temporarily moved the police station to a ticket booth at Sir Vivian Richards Stadium because of the demolition of the old station. When they walked the short distance, they found the stadium locked. They sat on the bench outside the stadium. Suzie suggested John call Jack, the Antiguan police officer who had last spoken with him. It was 2 AM, so it surprised John when he picked up the call on the second ring.

"We found Rick," said John. John described what had happened in the anchorage of Great Bird Island. After John summarized the events, there was silence on the other end of the line. Antigua was a small, peaceful country. Acts of violence, such as those described, were very unusual. The Island's economy was based on tourism, and every Antiguan knew how vulnerable they were to a single negative experience in the press. It could devastate their way of living.

"I am on my way," said Jack. "Meet me at the beach. It is faster by boat than driving on the roads."

John, Bev, Debbie, and Suzie were sitting on the sand at the beach when Jack arrived 20 minutes later. He pulled his boat as close to the beach as possible and jumped into knee-deep water. He tied the boat's dock line onto a rock. Jack could see that the four of them were mentally and physically exhausted and were having difficulty staying awake. Jack took a brief statement from John before calling for a taxi to take them to the closest hotel, Nonsuch Bay Hotel.

When the taxi arrived, he said, "We'll talk more tomorrow. I will send a car to the hotel to pick you up around 11 AM to bring you to the station. I will need an official statement from each of you."

John thanked him as the four of them sat in the taxi. The hotel was not full, and they registered in three rooms. When John closed the door, he stripped and went into the shower. His singed hair was in knots. He smelled like gasoline and soot. Even after scrubbing for 15 minutes, he could not remove the stench. He collapsed on the bed and fell asleep when his head hit the pillow.

The following day, a police van picked them up at 11 AM. They drove them to St. John's, the capital of Antigua. At the police precinct, four different officers took each of their statements. It took two hours. Jack mentioned to John he had spoken with Sidney Noseworthy. Jack suggested John contact him when he returned to Toronto.

"You need to leave the island," Jack told the four of them after taking their statements. "We have booked your return flights to Toronto for this evening."

A police cruiser drove them directly to the airport and helped with the check-in process with WestJet. Before they knew what had happened, they sat in their seats, flying back to Toronto.

That was yesterday. Today, they were telling the same story to the police in Toronto.

Sidney returned to the room where John was sitting with the coffee. "I spoke with the other officers who interviewed the rest of your crew. Their stories are consistent with yours. Where I am having problems is understanding why someone would go to all this effort to kill you. I think you mistakenly manufactured evidence to fit your delusion that someone is out to get you. I checked with the legal department. All the information you gave us from sleuthing on the dark web and finding the Bitcoin transaction occurring on the computer in Nigel's apartment is too farfetched to believe. In legal terms, you illegally got the information. We cannot use it. I caution you about invading privacy in this digital world we live in. John, you cannot hack into other people's computers and expect us to make a case."

John stared at Sidney incredulously. "That's ridiculous!" John cried out. He was trying to keep control of his rising anger.

"Someone strangled Joe Sawchuk, fracturing his larynx, then went to extraordinary lengths to make it look like an accident. Then they did a hit-and-run murder of the pathologist who was on his way here to report that Joe's death was not accidental. I got my privileges suspended from the hospital when I tried to expose the truth. Rick tried to kill me while scuba diving, then blew up my boat. Yet you say there is no case?"

"You need to step back and look at the evidence," said Sidney. He held up the pathology report. "It says here Joe's death was an accident and alcohol related. There is nothing written here about a fractured larynx. Your pathologist friend Derek was in the parking lot of a drinking establishment. It is not the first hit and run by a drunk driver in this parking lot. His story is buried with him, so we will never know what he was going to tell us.

"They suspended your hospital privileges after a hearing from your peers, not just this Nigel person. As far as Rick goes, the way I see it, he was on a personal vendetta. He threatened you in Toronto as well. There is no bigger conspiracy such as you have alluded to. Surfing on the dark web to look for evidence, I expect that action from a desperate man. Suzie told us about your wife filing for divorce. This can drive the most sensible men over the edge, distort cognitive function, and alter perceptions about reality.

"I see a broken surgeon before me, trying to blame everyone else for his problems. If I arrested every person in a leadership position who gets accused of nefarious activities by a well-meaning citizen espousing paranoid theories, there would be no politicians or leaders left."

John put his head in his hands and looked down at the table. This could not be happening. The truth was no longer important to Sidney. Sidney was looking for a common thread that would explain the events so he could tie them together neatly in a perfect bow. His 'broken surgeon' theory pieced everything together in a way that required no further investigation from him. John knew that anything else he said would prove to Sidney that his 'broken surgeon' theory was correct.

John stood up from the table and walked out of the interrogation room and left the precinct.

Chapter 29

Nigel was pacing in his living room. The beautiful view of Lake Ontario, with the soft snow falling and the reflection in the lake of the brightly lit CN Tower, went unnoticed. He was in a rage. "You said your plan was foolproof. Tomorrow, I will meet with the board, and John will accuse me of tainting his suspension process. How am I going to convince them otherwise?"

Rebecca regarded him and thought about how he was dealing with the stress. Whenever there was a problem, he turned into a raging orator. She knew he must learn how to control his outbursts if he was going to be successful in his new position. Perhaps he was only like this with her? If so, she could deal with that. She realized she would have to work with him so he could learn ways to control his temper.

"No one is going to believe what John has to say," she replied. "You heard what Sidney Noseworthy said about John being a 'broken surgeon'. He does not believe that business about the bitcoin coming from my computer and the other nonsense that John fed him about the dark web sites. It was I who sent him the pathology report anonymously. I also sent him the minutes of the Medical Advisory Meeting discussing his suspension."

Nigel listened patiently. There was more to the story than she was telling him. "I need to know what you have been up to," said Nigel quietly. "Is it true you hacked into John's identity to buy $32,000 of bitcoin and then used that to pay Rick to make John's death look like an accident?"

"There are certain things you are better off not knowing," replied Rebecca.

"You did it, didn't you!" shouted Nigel. "I need to know!"

Rebecca went quiet. She got up, walked to the floor-to-ceiling window, and looked at the magnificent view. The snow was falling with thicker flakes now. They were obscuring the view of the lake. It was completely quiet outside, with the snow buffering the distant sound of traffic twenty-four floors below. She would have to tell him sometime. Rebecca needed to explain to him why it was so important for her he get the position of Deputy Minister of Health. She hoped she could gently break it to him over the coming year, a little at a time. Whether Nigel knew it, he was in deep with her business. He had paid $20,000 to have Joe Sawchuk killed. Although he could deny he knew anything about it, he could not deny the $20,000 that left his account and ended up in Rick's account.

Without turning around, she said quietly, "Yes, it was me."

Nigel did not respond. He stared at her back. She was wearing a long black dress that hugged her perfect contours. Her thick black hair hung to her mid-back. Her narrow waist led to perfect hips and her beautifully sculpted buttocks. Long legs appeared below the hem of the skirt. Small, perfect feet supported the entire frame. He imagined her naked, standing before the window with the soft snow falling. How could someone so perfect do something so unimaginable?

"Why?" was all that came out when he spoke.

Rebecca turned around and approached him. She took his hand and led him to the sofa. They sat down beside each other. She told him the story about her grandfather and the 'accidental' death of the surgeon. She explained the business that generated millions of dollars annually for her and her family. The process of obtaining clients by befriending lonely and poorly paid night nurses, she rationalized to Nigel, was doing the healthcare system a favor by offering support to angry and grieving families. Using the dark web to send information to clients and receive payments by bitcoin was untraceable. It had been 10 years since she set up the system, and business was booming.

"In Canada," she continued, "only about 7% of lawsuits against doctors result in payments to harmed patients and their families. Many of the plaintiffs embark on litigation out of anger and spite. They want to punish the doctor. For most of them, it is not about getting money. They want revenge. There are tremendous opportunities to expand the business into Canada and help these grieving families get the justice they deserve. Accidents happen every day. No one will notice one or two more accidents involving incompetent doctors. The patients and their families can pay lawyers who will probably lose the lawsuit or pay us, knowing they will get justice."

Nigel listened while she told the story. Although he would never tell her, he agreed with her. He expected a medical world of perfection. Nigel had always believed no one should tolerate surgeons making mistakes or botching operations. He could never understand how they got away with bad outcomes without getting punished. Rebecca described it as though they were doing society a favor by her system. It had worked well in China. It could work well here.

"What does this do with me being the Deputy Minister of Health?" asked Nigel.

Rebecca had not worked out all the details yet, but her overall plan was in place. "We have ready access to coroner's reports in the Ontario Ministry of Health, so we will know when a surgical misadventure has occurred. I will not rely on lonely, poorly paid night nurses to find clients. We could have a grief counselor approach the potential clients to determine if their anger might be enough for them to want justice. We would then switch to the dark web for the rest of the transaction.

"The Ontario Ministry of Health has the most secure internet in the world. We would tap into that security, and this would protect us from getting caught. Within 3 years, we will have over ten million in Bitcoin, which is when we leave the country. This is just the start. We could expand to other countries. This could be a one hundred-million-dollar business within a few years."

Nigel's head was spinning. He knew he deserved to have this kind of revenue. There was always something to remind him he was smarter and better than everyone else around him. Being with Rebecca was another reminder of his natural superiority. She was beautiful, smart, and the envy of everyone she met. The perfect partner for the perfect man. He was a born leader, but he also knew this would never get him rich unless he directed his talents toward his financial security. This business would not only be doing the world a tremendous service but would also get him the financial security he deserved.

"Nigel?" asked Rebecca, "have I said too much?"

Nigel looked at her and smiled. "My role in this would be to look the other way?" he asked. "They would give me the highest internet security you could use to conduct business. It sounds like there would be little risk of getting caught. I am going to think about all of this."

The Complication

Rebecca leaned over and kissed him. She slid her tongue into his mouth. Sliding on top of him, she pulled up her skirt and rubbed herself against Nigel. She was not wearing panties.

Five miles away, behind a closed door in another part of Toronto, Ainslie and Adrian listened to the moaning and pleasurable sounds coming from the sofa in suite 2401.

"I guess that is why my dad said not to invade someone's privacy," said Ainslie as she stopped the recording and turned off the sound.

"I was not expecting that," said Adrian. "I don't mean the sex, and I mean the business of doctors meeting their accidental death at the hands of Rebecca,"

"My dad is extremely lucky to still be alive!" exclaimed Ainslie. "We recorded them admitting they tried to kill him, and they were the ones who tapped into his identity. I can't believe this."

"What are we going to do with this?" asked Adrian.

Ainslie went quiet. "My dad told me what they said to him about invading privacy at the police station. The police cannot use this material."

Adrian thought back to Ainslie's dad's suggestion that he try to find out whether the dark web sites with the menu of services could be connected to the laptop in suite 2401. Adrian traced the links from the Bitcoin transaction to Rebecca's laptop. He did not find any connection to those dark websites but accessed the audio and video components of the laptop. He arranged the setup to record anything happening in the apartment on Ainslie's computer. The laptop offered only a partial view of the living room, and when Nigel was pacing back and forth, they would see him just as he was turning around to pace the other way. The sofa was out of view, but they could hear everything.

"If your dad finds out what we did, will he be mad?" asked Adrian.

Before Ainslie could answer, there was a knock on her door. "Honey," asked John, "Can I come in?"

"We will find out soon enough," said Ainslie to Adrian.

"Come on in, Dad," she shouted. "We have something to show you."

Chapter 30

John was in the boardroom. Sitting beside him was his lawyer, Tracy. Nigel was at the other end of the boardroom table with a confident smirk. John avoided looking at him. The twelve board members were sitting around the room engaged in quiet conversation before the meeting started. John looked around the room. The hospital lawyer, David Wilkins, was sitting next to Nigel and turned to say something to him. The board members were all prominent businesspeople or community leaders. They volunteered to be board members of the hospital for altruistic reasons. They wanted to help with the management of the hospital and the lives of those who lived in the surrounding underprivileged community. The board members gave the hospital their business management knowledge as a gift. The meeting had only one agenda item- the suspension of Dr. John Hegland.

"Let's get started," said the chair of the board, Les Garvey. Les was the CEO and president of the largest car dealership in Toronto. His business was only a few blocks away from the hospital, and it was his practice to give good deals to the staff at the hospital. He was in his late 60s and had thick, wavy hair. He had a deep tan from a recent visit to St. Barts, where he kept his 75-foot motor yacht moored for the season.

The Complication

His passion for the healthcare system resulted from when his wife had breast cancer. He watched as she shriveled to 80 lbs. The metastasis was unresponsive to the 6 months of chemotherapy. When she died, there was an empty void in his life. However, he found the nurses and the doctors looking after her were compassionate and kind. He developed a bond with the cancer care clinic, and although she died from the cancer, he knew the team had tried their best. Many of the staff who looked after her attended her funeral and cried with him. He vowed to do whatever he could to give back to the healthcare system with the same passion and kindness the healthcare system had given him.

His skills were all business-related. He would not tolerate incompetence. He prided himself on being an excellent judge of character. The ability to read people and their motives came from 40 years of running a successful car dealership. He survived when many other dealerships around him failed because he could tell when someone tried to take advantage of him.

The boardroom became quiet. "This is a special board meeting," said Les, "to discuss the suspension of Dr. John Hegland by the Medical Advisory Committee. John has requested the board to review the decision. The board must decide on two aspects regarding the suspension. First, we must determine if the suspension process was fair, and the second is to determine if the decision was just."

The chair of the board looked around the room. "Everyone has seen the material sent around ahead of time. I will first ask John to speak. The next speaker will be Nigel. After that, John can speak again. After that, anyone can ask either of them questions for clarification. Once we finish the questions, I will ask both Nigel and John to leave the hearing so we can deliberate. In keeping with bylaws, we will not permit either lawyer to speak except to clarify a legal position."

The chair looked around the room again to see if anyone had questions. Seeing none, he said, "Should we start with you, John?"

John stood up. He looked around the room. Everyone was quiet. "Thank you for allowing me this hearing. I will start by giving you the timeline and explaining my actions. I believe that there has been a misunderstanding of the events. As I relate the events, I want you to remember that I witnessed what happened, so you will see it from my eyes."

John started with the complication, the ambulance ride, and the death of the patient. He discussed the angry family and Joe Sawchuk's death. John discussed his relationship with the coroner's office and Derek's autopsy findings of strangulation. He discussed the death of Derek and his subsequent visits with the police. The narrative took about 30 minutes.

"I know in my heart I have done nothing that deserves suspension. I was doing my job as chief of surgery to get to the truth of what happened," ended John.

Nigel stood up. He took his time to look at everyone directly into their eyes in the room. He was puffing out his chest and had his hands on his hips as if to tell the room that this was his meeting and that he was in charge. His arrogant smile was to let the room know that he would not let them believe the nonsense John had fed them.

"I'll start by saying that is the biggest load of crap I have heard in a while. After all the damage caused by John, he still dares to stand in front of this distinguished and honorable group to tell you lies. He had no right to go to the coroner's office under the pretense of the hospital's authority. Joe Sawchuk's autopsy report is in your package, and there is nothing about a fractured larynx or ruptured blood vessels in the whites of his eyes compatible with strangulation. A drunk driver killed Derek, so we will never know what he told John. He completely fabricated his stories to save his skin. In the words of one of the most thorough and honest police detectives, Sidney Noseworthy, I quote, 'He is a broken surgeon'. You have the Medical Advisory meeting minutes, so I won't repeat all that except that most of the chiefs agreed with me that his behavior was unprofessional and deserved a suspension."

The board members looked at John as he stood up to speak. "Thank you for allowing me to speak again." John looked around the room, wondering whether the board members believed him or Nigel. Their faces were expressionless, giving away nothing. "Before the Medical advisory meeting, I believe Nigel spoke with the chiefs individually about suspending me. He left some of them with the impression that if they did not support him at the meeting, the same fate would happen to them. Our by-laws on page 88, state in bold letters that, for the process to remain fair and impartial, no one must discuss the case before the meeting. I believe he tainted the process by intimidating the chiefs."

Nigel bolted to his feet. "That is complete bullshit! How dare you drag my integrity through the mud? I'm certain the board sees through your paranoid delusions. This is exactly the reason John needs to be suspended. He is unfit to practice." Nigel's face was red and the veins in his face were bulging as he sat down. His eyes were piercing right through John.

Tracy turned to the chair and put her hand up. "May I address the chair on a legal point?"

Les glanced at the hospital lawyer, who nodded and said, "Yes, let's hear it."

"To find out who is telling the truth, we would like to ask one of the members of the Medical Advisory committee to give a statement here," said Tracy.

Nigel leaped to his feet again and shouted, "That is highly irregular! We cannot allow it! I am the chair of the Medical Advisory Meeting, and I am the one to report to the board."

The chair looked at Nigel incredulously and said, "Nigel, sit down. Before you speak, you need my permission. I am the chair of the board! This is not your meeting!" Les turned to his lawyer and said, "David, would Tracy's request be in order?"

"In such a hearing, it is up to the chair to decide," replied David. "My opinion would be to allow it because the allegation needs to be clarified."

Les thought about it for a moment before he said, "I'm going to allow the Medical Advisory committee member to speak to us."

Tracy got up from the table and walked back a moment later with Jamie Spritz, the president of the medical staff association. Nigel glared at Jamie as he walked in. Jamie glanced at Nigel, and in that moment, John could see fear in his eyes. The moment passed, and Jamie sat down.

Les looked at Jamie kindly and said, "Thanks for coming to the hearing. I assume you know what this is about, so please go ahead."

Jamie cleared his throat and put his hands on the table before him. His fingers were banging together in front of him in a nervous tic. He locked his fingers together to stop the movement. "Nigel called me the day before the meeting to tell me about the proposed suspension of John. I knew nothing about it, so he explained John was delusional and causing harm to the hospital. He needed to be stopped. He said he expected me to support him. I told him it seemed draconian, and the suspension was too drastic. I didn't think I could support it. He said he had been through my medical file. He asked if I wanted everyone to know about my suicide attempt 3 years ago. After that, I felt confused. I should never have supported the suspension."

"That's a lie!" roared Nigel. "No one here will believe that!" He was standing up, pointing his finger at Jamie. He was breathing in quick motions, and his face was bright red.

"If you speak out of turn again," shouted Les, "I will ask you to leave the meeting."

Nigel shook his head as he sat down. Tracy put up her hand.

"Yes, you may speak," said Les.

"I have 3 other members of the Medical Advisory Committee sitting in the hallway outside the boardroom who are prepared to give similar statements to the board," said Tracy.

Les looked around the room. Nigel was glaring at him. Les had dealings with many types of people during his business career. He now had a good sense about Nigel. Narcissistic, dishonest, shameless, and a bully all came to mind simultaneously. "As chair, I do not think we need to hear anything else. Perhaps now would be a good time for John, Nigel, and Tracy to leave so we can deliberate."

Nigel got up, knocking his chair backward, so it fell over. He stormed out of the room, not picking up the fallen chair. John and Tracy gathered their notes and quietly sat in a small office next to the boardroom. They discussed how the meeting had gone, but in less than 5 minutes, there was a knock at the door. The record keeper said, "They have finished their deliberations. You can come back inside the boardroom."

John and Tracy sat in their seats. The record keeper went to Les and whispered something in his ear, then sat down in her place beside him. Les said, "Unfortunately, Nigel has left the building so that we will continue without him. After hearing the statements, the board unanimously decided to reinstate your privileges. On behalf of the board, I apologize for any inconvenience this has caused."

John breathed an enormous sigh of relief. His 'broken surgeon' image was mending itself, and this was just the beginning.

Chapter 31

Nigel hung up the phone. He was standing in his penthouse apartment, looking out of the window. The call was from Les Garvey, the board of directors' chair. Les wanted him to tender his resignation immediately. As he was moving into the Deputy Minister of Health position in less than a month, that would not be a problem. Les suggested that no further investigation into his ill-fated Medical Advisory meeting would occur if he resigned immediately. This might work in Nigel's favor. Nigel's attempt to suspend a disruptive physician would be portrayed as being thwarted by a left-leaning board of directors who showed leniency towards disciplining doctors.

"Did you lose your temper at the meeting?" asked Rebecca. Nigel turned around to face Rebecca and smiled.

"I could not contain myself," admitted Nigel. "You would not believe the bullshit that flowed out of the meeting." Nigel laughed as he thought back to the nervous wreck of the president of the medical staff association. "You should have seen Jamie shake like a leaf before he talked to the board. What a wimp. It is good to see I have so much control over these assholes."

"So, you will send your resignation, citing irreconcilable ideological differences?" asked Rebecca.

"It will be a long email portraying me as a knight in shining armor out to rid the world of bad doctors," answered Nigel. "The board of directors will be the sniveling socialist weaklings, afraid to do what is right. I think this will be beneficial to us."

"What do you think we should do about John?" asked Rebecca.

Nigel thought about that for a moment. John had been a huge disruption to his plans. The suspension was to remove him from the picture, so he had a clear path to the Deputy Minister of Health position. Now that he had the job, there was little he could do to disrupt that plan. "I think I would let it go now. Most of us in leadership positions have created enemies along the way. John is just another in my long line of enemies. There is little he could do now to harm me."

"I wouldn't be so certain," replied Rebecca. "I suspect he is one of those who subscribe to the motto, 'What doesn't kill me makes me stronger.' I do not think we have seen the last of him. I think it would be important for us to tie up loose ends. He knows we are the ones who stole his identity and paid $32,000 in Bitcoin to Rick. That may come back to haunt us."

"What are you suggesting?" asked Nigel.

"I've hired my main man in China to pay John a visit," explained Rebecca. "He has created over 1000 'accidents' in China and is a master of deception and is like a ghost. No one will even know he was here."

"That's way too risky!" said Nigel. "I say we let it go and take our chances of leaving him alone."

"It's too late," said Rebecca. "Once we strike the deal, there is no way to cancel it. That is the beauty of the system. We do not contact him, and he has no contact with us. We'll hear about his 'accident' in the news or through the hospital. He's leaving tonight to come to Toronto. You will thank me in a few days."

Ainslie's eyes felt like they would pop out of her head as she listened to what Rebecca had said. "Oh my God," Ainslie cried out. She was sitting in front of her computer with her dad and Adrian in her room. John had told Ainslie about the board meeting earlier that evening, and he expected Nigel to retaliate in some fashion. Adrian had set up the recordings to occur when a movement or a voice was detected. John had not expected to be targeted by an imported accident expert.

"We know what will happen if we get to the police with this," said Ainslie. "Absolutely nothing. That Noseworthy detective will probably put us in jail for invading the privacy of these upstanding citizens. I think we are on our own here."

"There is no 'we'," said John. "You and Claudia are going to your Gramma's house. One of the 'accidents' might be a house fire."

Adrian was banging away on his laptop. After a minute, he spoke. "The most common accidental death in Ontario is from a motor vehicle accident, not a house fire," he said. "A house fire is too dramatic and would cause unnecessary investigations. He would want you to die in an automobile accident. He will most likely cause the car to turn off the road by damaging the brakes or, more likely, loosening the bolts from your car tires. That way, a tire will fly off at high speeds, and you will crash into something."

John thought about this for a moment. Adrian was right. The purpose of calling in this 'accident' expert was so that the death would not draw attention. A further internet search revealed there were 74,000 car accidents last year in Ontario, with 359 deaths. Someone would not likely notice one more death, especially if it appeared to be an accidental failure of some part of the car. John knew little about cars or how to disable them. He needed to find someone who could advise him. A thought flashed through his mind. He picked up his phone and punched in a number.

"Excuse me for a minute, kids," he said. John left them in Ainslie's room. He walked down the stairs and into his study.

"Suzie," he said on the phone. "Can you come over? I need to talk to you. Can you bring your brother, Marco?"

Marco was Suzie's older brother. He had been in Canada longer than Suzie, over 10 years. John did not know all the details, but at some point in his life, he was a member of FARC, the Revolutionary Armed Forces of Colombia. The details of his escape from Colombia and into Canada were unknown to John. When Suzie talked about him, she said he was the best car mechanic in the city. John wanted to talk to him about what an 'accidental' death from an automobile might look like.

An hour later, Suzie arrived with her brother, Marco. John met him once when Suzie invited him to the boat for race night. The sailing race was a disaster for him. He vomited from the moment the boat left the dock until it returned. He had not stepped on a boat of any kind since then. Marco was short but stocky. He had thick muscles on his arms and legs. He cut his hair short, but he had a thick beard. His eyes were dark and piercing. They darted around the entrance of the house as if looking to assess whether there was any danger.

Suzie hugged John as soon as she got through the door. She squeezed him tightly and buried her head in his shoulders. She had tears running down her cheeks and onto his shirt. "I was so worried about you. The police interrogation was awful. I could tell they didn't believe the story about Rick."

She suddenly disengaged from the prolonged hug and looked up at John and into his eyes. "What happened at the board meeting?"

"They re-instated my hospital privileges," said John gleefully. "I am no longer suspended."

Suzie leaned over and kissed him on the lips. John felt a shudder go through his body as he closed his eyes. The kiss lasted for 3 seconds but seemed to linger. He could smell her freshly washed hair, and she smelled like fresh flowers. He looked at her, keeping one arm on her shoulder, and said, "Come upstairs to Ainslie's room. I want to show you both something."

They were sitting on the edge of Ainslie's bed, watching the videos and listening to the conversations recorded between Rebecca and Nigel. Marco fixed his gaze on the computer screen, saying nothing. Suzie watched quietly and was the first to speak. "This is exactly what you said happened, and Sidney Noseworthy did not believe a word of it. They are still planning for you to have an accident. What are you going to do?"

"I cannot take this to the police," said John. "Sidney has warned me not to invade the privacy of others. I suspect he would still label me as a 'broken surgeon'. This is the reason I asked you to bring Marco. If an accident were to occur, likely it would involve my vehicle mechanically failing. I was hoping Marco could tell me what are some mechanisms that might cause a car to crash so I could be ready."

Marco did not reply. He thought about what he had seen on the recordings, and it was almost as if the others in the room could hear him thinking.

"I can do better than that," he whispered.

Chapter 32

John kissed Ainslie goodnight on the top of her head. "Don't stay up late again!" said John as he walked out of her room. It had been 24 hours since they reviewed the videos. They had stayed until the early hours of the morning, working on a plan. Marco explained he had been involved with the FARC, the revolutionary army in Colombia. He was the leader of the group that was involved in negotiating with the Colombian government for a peace accord. In the early part of the negotiations, some rebels opposed the peace accord and threatened Marco's life. Canada offered him refuge. In 2016, when the government and the rebels signed the agreement, he had already adapted to life in Canada and chose to stay rather than return to his home country of Colombia.

The FARC was involved in drug trafficking to finance the militia. Other activities included kidnapping for ransom, bombing government targets, and terrorism. Terrorism was Marco's area of expertise. After discussing all the possibilities and potential risks, Marco spent the day at John's house preparing. From the review of the video and audio recordings of Rebecca and Nigel, the impression was that the 'accident' would occur within a few days. They needed to move quickly.

John was asleep at 2 AM when the explosion happened. It shook the house and startled him as he woke up. John leaped out of bed and raced to the driveway where he had parked his car. The car was on fire. Next to the car, but 30 feet away from the developing inferno, was an oriental man who was unconscious. His right arm was missing, and blood was spurting out of the axillary artery. There was a stump of his upper arm remaining. John rapidly took off his pajama top and rolled it into a ball to apply pressure. The direct pressure applied to the open artery controlled the bleeding.

Ainslie and her sister Claudia rushed out to see what had happened. Seeing their dad covered in blood, they both screamed at the top of their lungs. John looked up at them and said, "I'm okay, kids. This man had his arm blown off, and I needed to control the bleeding. I want you both to go inside and call 911." Ainslie and Claudia rushed back into the house, and each made the call on their cellphones.

Neighbors appeared and formed a circle around John as he applied pressure to the bleeding artery. Some with cellphones were placing their own calls to 911. They stayed away from the burning car, fearing it might explode. Even though John was kneeling in front of the man thirty feet from the car, he could feel the heat on his back as the fire grew in intensity.

John heard the sirens in the distance. The fire truck was the first to arrive and quickly doused the flames from the burning car. The ambulance was next. John continued to press on the artery to stop the bleeding. He helped the paramedics load the unconscious man into the ambulance and accompanied the ambulance to the closest trauma hospital. John knew the resident of the trauma team, Sarah, as she had just finished a rotation at John's hospital.

"There was an explosion which blew off his right arm," John explained.

"Where's the arm?" asked Sarah.

"Not sure," answered John. "It was probably incinerated in the explosion. The axillary artery is actively bleeding. I can help you ligate the artery and vein here in the emergency room. That way, we'll have time to do CAT scans to make sure there are no other injuries."

Sarah ran off to get a minor suture kit. She returned and put on some surgical gloves while John maintained pressure on the artery. They traded positions, so John put on some surgical gloves while Sarah pushed on the artery. Once they were ready, Sarah released the pressure. John soaked the area with Betadine, and the two of them quickly clamped the bleeding artery. It took less than a minute to put a ligature around the vessel. The axillary vein had retracted deep into the axilla. John separated the damaged tissues with surgical retractors so that Sarah could reach into the depths and grab the bleeding axillary vein. She sutured the end of the vein. The bleeding had stopped. Sarah carefully cleaned the wound and placed a dressing. They now had time to do further tests before taking him to the operating room to close the wound.

They did CAT scans of his head, chest, and abdomen and determined there were no other injuries. By the time he regained consciousness, the police had arrived. The injured man refused to say anything. He refused to allow them to take him to surgery, so they took him to the surgical ward.

John explained to the police officer, "He is an assassin. They sent this man from China to make me have an accident. He is a criminal." The police officer called his supervisor, who advised cuffing the assassin to the hospital bed and keeping a 24-hour guard until they could sort it out.

John washed his hands. He watched as the blood from his hands and arms washed away down the drain. While he was drying his hands, he heard a police officer say, "You need to come to the precinct with us for questioning."

John followed the police officer to his car and sat in the back seat. They took him into a familiar interrogation room, where he sat on a hard wooden chair and waited. It was 4 AM, but adrenaline was pumping through his body. He did not expect Marco's work to have done so much damage. It surprised him that the explosion blew his car up and tore the arm off the assassin. He was thinking about how much to tell the police when Sidney Noseworthy walked in.

Sidney looked at John. The hospital had given John a patient gown, but he was still wearing his pajama bottoms. There were blue paper slippers from the hospital on his feet. Sidney sat down in front of John and said, "Are you okay with us recording this?"

John said it was okay to record. John told him about the board meeting, which resulted in his suspension being lifted. He explained how he had recorded Nigel and Rebecca discussing how they had paid Rick with the bitcoin. The last conversation about bringing an accident specialist from China caused Sid to raise his eyebrows. Finally, John explained how he needed to protect himself, which resulted in the explosion.

"You told me not to invade their privacy the last time we met," said John. "If I had brought you the tapes, you would have discarded them and told me I was paranoid. There was nowhere for me to turn, so I took matters into my own hands."

Sidney stopped taking notes and contemplated John. "This has gone way too far. I do not know what to believe anymore. What I am seeing is a paranoid, broken surgeon blowing up someone who was likely a car thief. This is not a society of vigilante justice. I am arresting you for attempted murder. You have the right to remain silent and may speak with your lawyer. I advise you not to say anything until you have legal advice."

Sidney walked around to John's side of the table and placed handcuffs. There were two police officers who had been watching through the one-way mirror who entered the room. They took John to a cell that had 10 other men. There was space for him to sit on a bench where two other men were sleeping, propped against the wall. The room was dark, with just enough light to see. It smelled of urine and vomit. Most of the men were sleeping on the floor, snoring loudly. There was one man talking quietly to the wall. He had no shoes on his feet, and his shirt, torn in several places, was covered in a thick, dirty film. He had long black hair in knots and a thick grey beard that hung to his chest. Every 5 minutes, he would yell something unintelligible at the wall and then go back to his constant muttering.

John sighed. Maybe he was just a "broken surgeon' after all.

Chapter 33

"John Hegland," shouted the prison guard.

John realized he must have drifted asleep. Opening his eyes brought him back to the reality of having been stuck in a jail cell overnight. He stood up and said, "That's me."

"Come with me," said the guard. John put his arms out, expecting the guard to place handcuffs. Instead, the guard said, "That will not be necessary."

The guard turned around. John followed him down the hallway and into the interrogation room. Sidney Noseworthy was sitting in front of his notes and the tape recorder, which was turned off. John wondered if he had ever slept. John sat in the chair in front of him. "You are free to go," he said. "I want you to stay in the city in case we need more information from you. Someone brought you some clothes. You can change in here before you leave."

Sidney passed him a brown paper bag, and then he got up from his chair and walked out the door. John stared at him as he was leaving, wondering what had just happened.

John opened the bag and removed the cargo pants. He put them over the top of his pajamas. The shirt was a clean white shirt someone had taken from his closet. He removed the dirty paper slippers they had given him at the hospital and replaced them with the clean socks and shoes that were in the bag. He walked out the door, and an officer directed him into the lobby of the precinct. Sitting on a chair near the door was Suzie. She jumped up and ran to John and embraced him.

"Thank God you are OK!" she said. "I cannot believe they made you spend the night in jail! Sidney gave me the excuse it was for your own protection while they checked out your story, but I don't believe him."

John looked at Suzie before speaking, "Let's get out of here before they change their minds."

They walked outside to a parking lot. Marco was sitting in his car. Suzie hopped into the back seat, and John got into the front seat. "We are driving you home," said Marco. John was quiet on the ride home. He needed some time to sort out what had happened. Was he still being charged with attempted murder? Should he call his lawyer? They pulled up into his driveway. His burned car was gone.

"They took it away for forensic testing," said Suzie, pointing to where the car had been. "I'm going to make you some breakfast. Then we are going to come up with a plan."

John got out of the car. Suzie and Marco followed him into the house. It was 7:00 in the morning, so he went upstairs and woke up Ainslie and Claudia. "Time to get ready for school," John said to Ainslie.

"Dad!" she shouted as she woke up. "You're here! What happened? Where were you all night?"

John said, "It's a long story. Can we catch up when you get home from school?" Ainslie reluctantly agreed. "Suzie is making us breakfast, so hurry."

John went into the second bedroom and woke up his other daughter, Claudia. "Time to get up, darling."

"Where did you go last night?" she asked.

"I'll tell you the long tale when you get home from school tonight," said John. "Breakfast is almost ready."

John went down the stairs to the kitchen. Suzie was making cheese omelets with onions and mushrooms. Buttered toast was on the table. A steaming cup of coffee was waiting for him. Marco was sitting next to him, drinking his coffee. He looked at John with concern in his eyes and said, "You are probably wondering what happened to your car."

John, still overwhelmed by the events, nodded his head.

Marco had a thick Hispanic accent despite his 10 years in Toronto. He was fidgeting with his hands in a nervous gesture. His eyes had softened as he looked at John. "The car was not supposed to catch fire and blow that guy's arm off," Marco explained. "I rigged things so that anyone who tried to tamper with the engine or brakes would get the shock of their lives, but it would not kill them. Tampering with the engine would trigger a device to lock the arm to the engine with a special clamp. I set up a similar trap if he tried to tamper with anything underneath the car. The plan would be to have him handcuffed to the car while the police came."

"What went wrong?" asked John.

Marco shook his head. "I used this in Colombia. There were some rebels who did not agree with a peace treaty with the government. I had rigged this up to my personal car because of death threats. In Colombia, a death threat meant they wanted to either shoot me or blow me up. I caught the guy who wanted to kill me. One morning, when I came to my car, he had handcuffed himself to my car with my trap."

"What happened to him?" asked John.

Marco went quiet. "At first, I wasn't sure what to do, so I called my commanding officer. He came to my house and shot him in the head. He said we needed to make an example of what would happen to others if they tried to derail the peace talks."

Suzie interrupted the conversation and placed the omelets in front of Marco and John. "Eat these while they are hot," she said. "Do your girls like cheese omelets? I am making some for them."

John smiled at Suzie and nodded. "They love omelets." Claudia and Ainslie walked into the kitchen and sat down.

"Dad, you need to tell us how that guy got his arm blown off last night," said Ainslie. "We are not getting on the bus to go to school until you tell us."

Marco looked at John. "It's okay, Marco," said John.

"The trap engaged as planned," said Marco. "The clamp immobilized the right arm onto the engine. I did not expect his right hand to be clutching C4 explosives. When the trap engaged, it must have triggered the detonator, which ignited the explosives and blew off his arm, throwing him 30 feet away. He is lucky to be alive.

"In his black bag next to him, the police found a GPS tracker, another detonator and more explosives. They believe the explosives were to be detonated while you were driving at 100 k/hr on the expressway. You would fly off the road and land 50 feet below in an explosion. No one would suspect it was deliberate."

Suzie said, "Ainslie called me after you went with the ambulance and told me what happened. Marco and I came over here and explained what we knew to the police officers who were milling around. They dragged us downtown for a grilling with Sidney Noseworthy." Suzie lifted her hands and turned them facing up. "And here we are."

Ainslie and Claudia were eating their omelets while listening intently. Finally, Ainslie spoke. "Dad, there is something I need to tell you. Do you know those tapes of Rebecca and Nigel? Well, I sent them to Fox news with an explanation. Anonymously, I explained how a hitman arrived from China to kill you. An explosion blew off his right arm. I said the police did not believe you."

The kitchen went silent. "Oh, look at the time, Claudia. We better catch our bus!" Claudia and Ainslie raced out of the kitchen, grabbing the lunches that John had made for them the night before.

John flipped on the TV news. Ashley, the blonde news reporter who had interviewed Nigel on past newscasts, was standing in front of his burned-out car. It was behind a chain-linked fence. "Here is the burned-out car of Dr. John Hegland. The attempt to plant explosives and blow up the car to make it look like an accident had failed last night. The would-be assassin blew off his right arm. His intended victim, Dr. John Hegland, saved the would-be assassin's life in a dramatic ambulance ride and life-saving surgery at the trauma hospital. The perpetrator remains in police custody at the hospital. The story does not end there. Back to Jason at the studio."

The image flipped back to the news studio, where Jason and another female breakfast studio host were sitting behind a desk. "This is just in from our sister station at Fox news. A conversation between the former chief of staff, Dr. Nigel Gilman and his partner, Rebecca, revealed the story is deeper than a simple carjacking as originally suggested by the police." An image on the TV cut to edited segments of the recordings made by Ainslie and Adrian. The first video shown was the segment where Rebecca admits to having a business killing doctors and making it look like an accident. The next video was a segment on hacking into John's identity and stealing $32,000 from his American Express card. Finally, the audio segment appeared, where they discussed how to tie up loose ends after John had an accident.

John, Marco and Suzie watched in silence as Jason and the female host discussed the implications. "They discuss further along in the recording how they would use the security of the Ontario Ministry of Health internet to conduct a business of killing doctors if I understand this correctly," said Jason.

"As incredible as it sounds, that is my take on this as well. The Minister of Health has called for a press conference later this afternoon. We could not contact Dr. Hegland, although the police say he is with them for his own protection until they can sort this out."

John turned off the TV. He looked at Suzie and Marco. "That explains why Sidney Noseworthy let me go," he said. "He knew about the recordings from Fox news."

"What do you think will happen now?" asked Suzie.

John shook his head as he thought about what could happen. He hoped they did not trace the recordings back to his house. People might raise questions about the legitimacy of the recordings. They illegally recorded the conversations, so if it were ever determined they were the ones who hacked into Rebecca's computer, would they get in legal trouble?

John wondered if they had arrested Nigel and Rebecca yet. "I want to check on something. Come upstairs to Ainslie's room." John logged into Ainslie's computer. He clicked on the file that would open Rebecca's laptop video and audio. There was a message saying the device was not connected. There was another icon in the file, Google Timeline. John clicked on that. The computer appeared on google maps. It was the map of the Island Airport.

"It looks like Nigel and Rebecca are making a run for it," exclaimed Suzie. "We need to stop them!"

John said, "There is nothing we can do. We are an hour away from the airport at this time of day. Let's call Sidney Noseworthy."

Marco said, "Bad idea. He is going to want to know how we got this information, and we'll have to admit we hacked into their Google Timeline. I say we leave it to the police to figure out they are making a run for it. We can find out where they went by following them on Google Timeline."

"Hmmm," murmured John, "As long as they are away from me and they cannot hurt me, I don't care where they go. I want to get my life back." John turned the computer off, and the three of them walked down the stairs and into the kitchen.

They were cleaning the kitchen after finishing breakfast when John heard the chime of the security system as the front door opened and then closed with a resounding bang. Loud footsteps from hard-soled shoes echoed in the front vestibule.

Into the kitchen walked Marie.

Chapter 34

Hans sat quietly while John told him what had happened since the last visit. Hans has had a successful psychiatric practice for 35 years and has heard some remarkable stories. What happened to John over the past few weeks struck him as one of the most remarkable. Hans' astonishment stemmed from his surprise that John was still alive. He had defeated death on at least four or five separate attempts on his life by committed killers. How was that possible?

"My concern regarding your near-death experiences," said Hans, "is that you will probably develop a degree of PTSD. It can present in several ways and might catch you off guard when it happens. You might be walking down the street, and a car horn goes off, sending you into a full-blown panic attack. You might have trouble sleeping or even concentrating. It is important for you to understand what is going on if these symptoms occur."

John considered this for a moment and then said, "So far, I've felt nothing like that. My worst negative emotions flooded me in that jail cell, where I almost agreed with Sidney Noseworthy that I was a 'broken surgeon.' That didn't last because Suzie rescued me from the prison, and now I feel like my old self."

"What is happening with your work?" asked Hans.

"Things are going well," said John. "They are treating me like a rockstar at the hospital. Everyone is saying they knew he was an evil person, and I was the only one to stand up to him. Many of my colleagues would like me to be the next chief of staff. They say I am calm when all around me is chaos. It was nice to hear people say positive things about me.

"I operated all day on Monday. The surgery went well, and the operating room staff could not do enough to please me. They were so kind. I had a surgery staff meeting on Monday night. When I walked into the room, all the surgeons stood up and started clapping their hands. It was like I was a returning war hero from a distant land."

"What's happening with Marie?" asked Hans.

John went quiet. He could feel his anxiety returning with the familiar chest tightness, and he felt short of breath. He could not find a comfortable position to place his hands. His eyes darted from the floor to the picture on the wall behind Hans. It was a picture of two Muskoka wooden chairs painted bright red. The chairs were empty and positioned overlooking a sandy beach leading to the bright blue ocean water. In the distance, a short way off the shore, was a sailboat at anchor. It was as if the chairs were inviting John to sit down and enjoy the peaceful view. Draped over the top of one chair was an arm whose hand had long nails painted bright red. The rest of the woman was out of the picture, leaving John to wonder who she was and what she looked like.

"Things are not good," replied John. John looked down at his hands. He locked them together so he could not move them.

Hans remained quiet so John could speak when he felt ready. After thirty more seconds of silence, John said, "She came home the morning the news reports broke of the car explosion. Suzie and her brother, Marco, were in the kitchen with me. Her first words were, 'Get the fuck out of my house. All of you.' She was yelling at the top of her lungs. I convinced Suzie and Marco to leave. I walked them out to their car. Suzie was worried about my safety. She said to survive all the murder attempts, only to be killed by a crazy woman didn't seem fitting." John smiled as he thought about Suzie and her concern for him.

"Marie said I had endangered her children and was unfit as a father," continued John. "She said if I did not leave immediately, she would call the police and tell them I assaulted her. I really had no choice. The police had not believed my story from the beginning and would be unlikely to believe me now. I packed my things and moved into a hotel near the hospital."

"What did your lawyer say about this?" asked Hans.

"I'm meeting with her tomorrow afternoon," said John. "I don't think there is much my lawyer can do now that I have left the house. She originally told me not to leave because it weakens my negotiating position, but now that I have moved out, I feel safer."

"That is a very mature and reasonable response to manage an unreasonable situation," said Hans. "How do you feel about Suzie?"

"I am a bit confused because I find her attractive, but I know if anything happened, I would feel guilty because I am still married. I think I'm not quite ready. What worries me most is making the same mistake I made with Marie. How could I be so wrong about her? What if my delusions about the kind of woman I want to be with persist, and I make the same bad choice?"

Hans stroked his beard pensively and considered what John said before he answered. "When you look back on your relationship with Marie, I'm sure there were some red flags that you ignored. You need to think about what they were and why you ignored them. Only then will you be able to know whether you are making the same bad choices? I would suggest you write your thoughts and keep them handy so you can reflect on them."

John's chest tightness disappeared. His breathing became easier. Looking up at the picture that was on the wall behind Hans, he could see himself sitting on the chair beside the woman with the long red nails. He imagined they were looking at their sailboat. Although John could not clearly see the face of the woman yet, he imagined the hand resting on his shoulder instead of the top of the chair. This thought comforted him. He felt hopeful he could carve out a new life and find happiness.

"I started to do that already," said John. "I have written three pages to date, and the memories still come flooding back. I am seeing some patterns and admonish myself for not reacting to these patterns sooner. It is helpful to write things down. Thanks for the brilliant advice. I am finding these sessions very helpful."

"See you next week then?" asked Hans.

John nodded. He walked out of Hans' office with renewed hope, thinking about the picture of the two empty chairs.

Chapter 35

The exhumation of Joe Sawchuk's body made the front page of the news and was the feature story of every news outlet in North America. The coroner's office ordered another autopsy after the chief coroner, Brian Wilson, admitted that Rebecca from the Ontario Ministry of Health asked him to change the autopsy report. She threatened to expose pictures of him having sex with multiple male partners. He was, to all appearances, happily married to his wife of 25 years with three adult children. The pictures would have destroyed him. Now, the truth was out; his wife had left him, and his children would no longer talk to him.

John was instrumental in the exhumation order. Two weeks earlier, he was sitting with the hospital CEO, Nancy, in her office. "We need to find the truth about Joe Sawchuk," said John. "We can only clear this terrible tragedy involving deception and dishonesty up by getting to the truth of how Joe died."

"I agree with you. How can we go about this?" asked Nancy.

"A lot of the information I have is from Rebecca's computer," said John. "Sidney Noseworthy says it has no value in the legal system because I got it illegally. It turns out they blackmailed the chief coroner into changing the autopsy report to make it look like an accident. I approached the chief coroner and gave him an ultimatum. Either he comes clean with changing the autopsy report, or I expose him to the press. Things spiraled from there. I spoke with the coroner's office after he resigned, and they agreed to perform a second autopsy. They are going to exhume the body in two weeks after they approve the permits."

"That is excellent," said Nancy. "Have you given any thought to becoming our next chief of staff?"

"That is something I need a few more weeks to decide," said John. "I'd like to see whether the new autopsy report confirms what Derek told me, that Joe died of strangulation. If that is the case, there will be a warrant for the arrest of Nigel for murder and obstruction of justice, and I will feel totally exonerated. I do not want to be the chief of staff until they have completed that process."

"There is something else I want to discuss with you," said Nancy. "The board feels responsible for the abysmal way the hospital treated you. They would like to compensate you for the damage. They would like to pay you $50,000. Perhaps you need some time to think about it."

"Look," said John, "I do not need time to think about this. It was the board who stood up to Nigel and reversed the suspension. I am grateful for the trust they had in me. When the suspension happened, I was on a planned holiday anyway, so there were no financial damages. If the board wants me to sign something so I do not cause them trouble later, I would be happy to do that, although it is unnecessary."

Nancy stared at John. "I told the board you would say that, but they insisted I offer it to you, anyway."

John was present during the autopsy, along with Nancy, Sidney Noseworthy and others from the Ontario Ministry of Health. The pathologist was Rudy Samson, who had worked at the coroner's office for the past 25 years. "Look at the larynx," Rudy said. "Derek had previously examined it, and you can see it is fractured. The lungs have no water in them. The sclera is difficult to interpret because of the deterioration with time, but there are ruptured vessels in the eyeball. This is consistent with Derek's report of death from strangulation. I analyzed the urine and blood samples that were taken at the first autopsy. They were negative for alcohol or drugs., so alcohol was not a factor in his death."

John breathed a sigh of relief. He thought back to a month ago when Ainslie called him. She said, "I know you told me not to do this, but Adrian and I are still recording what Rebecca and Nigel are up to. They are making a good living out of causing accidents to doctors in China. On Google Timeline, we see they are in the Dominican Republic near Rincon on the beach. Dad, we needed to stop them."

"Honey, we cannot use the information because of how we got it," said John.

"I disagree," said Ainslie. She told John about the blackmail of Brian Wilson, the chief coroner. "Adrian found some deleted emails describing the blackmail, although we did not look for the pictures. Even if they charge Nigel with murder in Canada, the Dominican Republic has no extradition treaty with Canada, so no one can arrest him."

John thought about this for a moment. "Is there any way you can alert the police in China about what is going on with the accidental deaths of the doctors?" he asked.

"Adrian and I are way ahead of you, Dad," she replied. "One of the best gamers on League of Nations is from China and is friends with Adrian. We sent him all the dark web information. He passed this on anonymously to the police. They have made many arrests, including fifteen from Rebecca's family. They have arrested all the assassins and have shut down the dark websites. The police have frozen the accounts that Rebecca and Nigel were using. It is all over the China news. I'll send you the links to the news articles. Dad, I'm worried. They will be desperate now."

John opened the links to the news articles while Ainslie remained on the phone call. Using Google Translate, he could read the articles. The news described the arrests after an anonymous tip.

The police set up sting operations throughout China over a two-week period and shut down the operation. Across China, there was a hotline organized to report threats to doctors. Assaults on the medical profession were to get a minimum of 5 years in prison. The Chinese government gave top priority to stopping the practice of retribution to surgeons who had patients with complications following surgery.

Other articles mentioned the connection with Toronto. The police were working with the Canadian government to investigate the Canadian government's role in these activities. There was a picture of the assassin with the story of how he had his arm blown off trying to plant explosives in the car of a prominent surgeon. They talked about how this Canadian surgeon was a friend of China, having visited many times to perform surgery and give lectures.

The Chinese assassin was still not talking with the police. The article described the many operations that were necessary to cover the end of the arm with muscle flaps and skin grafts, all at the expense of the Canadian taxpayer. There was a trial planned in a few months, but he refused to talk with the court-appointed lawyer.

There was another news headline, "China to impose trade sanctions against Canada." The article described the rising political tensions between the governments of China and Canada. China accused the Canadian government of not doing enough to curtail illegal activity against Chinese citizens. Canada accused China of sending an assassin to harm one of their citizens. They were sending verbal volleys, threatening to pull their ambassadors. The secretary of state from the United States offered to be a mediator, but both China and Canada did not want him involved. The scandal was becoming a major international incident.

"I think we are safe, honey," said John as Ainslie had been patiently waiting on the phone. "Going after us will only cause them more grief."

"Dad, they said they will start the same business in Toronto now they have shut down the China operation," said Ainslie. "I have the recordings."

John went quiet. The first 'accident' might be for him.

Chapter 36

The sun was setting. The entire sky was lit by brilliant orange and pink colors that were reflecting off the calm waters in the bay. A slight breeze off the water felt cool after the heat from a day of unrelenting Caribbean sun. The beauty of the sunset and the quiet sound of the small waves that washed onto the sandy beach were the peace that they had been searching for. They knew the peace would only last for a few minutes while the sun was setting. They were sitting on the veranda of their condominium overlooking the ocean, sharing a bottle of chilled white wine. Once the darkness arrived, the stress of the previous few months would return with a vengeance.

Rebecca and Nigel knew they were in a major predicament, with only a few options left. When they left Toronto, they had to quickly pack and abandon most of their possessions. They had a few clothes, Rebecca's laptop, their passports and their wallets. Any money in their bank accounts, they changed into bitcoin when they arrived in the Dominican Republic. Since then, the police seized their bank accounts and their condominium. This effectively froze their Canadian assets.

Ashley, the news reporter, called Nigel early in the morning the day the story broke and asked him for comments about his involvement. He hung up on her. Rebecca and Nigel realized they only had a few hours to make their move. They hired a private jet out of the Island Airport and flew to Samana, in the Dominican Republic. They planned to continue operations from there. At first, things seemed to work well, and money was flowing into their accounts from the accidents they had organized in China. Then, disaster struck.

They found out a week ago the authorities arrested Rebecca's family, including her uncle Quan and her cousin Jessica. The authorities arrested the team of hitmen they had carefully selected over the past 10 years. They shut down their websites. They dismantled the payment system. The business was effectively closed.

"I don't believe what has happened," said Rebecca. "Nigel, someone has sold us out. Someone shut all the websites and gave evidence to the police in China. Who would do this?"

"It must have been someone in your family," said Nigel. "They are the only ones who knew the system."

"That is preposterous," said Rebecca. "There is no way they would jeopardize their livelihood. They have been doing the work for years with no hint of problems. The business could have continued for years but for you. The only change in the business plan has been to bring you into the fold so we could expand into Canada. Before that, we had no problems. You were the one who brought

John Hegland into the picture. He was the one who brought us down, and you failed to take of that problem."

"What are you talking about?" shouted Nigel. "You said you would take care of him. The wheels fell off when your incompetent assassin blew off his arm. It's all your fault. They froze our assets. We are going to run out of money within the next few weeks, thanks to you and your incompetent team. What the hell are we going to do now?"

Nigel was pacing back and forth. His face was bright red, and he focused his eyes on Rebecca. She threw his promising career down the drain. It was all her fault. Why he got involved with Rebecca, the psychopathic killer, was beyond him. She seduced him, which clouded his judgment. Now, he was a wanted criminal. The wealth he envisioned had slipped away. The situation was hopeless. They were stuck in this humid sweat factory of a country, and he could see no way out.

"I have a plan," said Rebecca calmly. "We know the system in Toronto. There are many disappointed patients and families. They want to avenge incompetent doctors, and I know how we can tap into their anger and profit. I set up a system before we had to leave. I have been working on this long before I met you. It is time to activate the plan."

A week had gone by, and the plan was falling into place. The plan she had been working on for years was going to pay big returns. Although she would prefer to oversee the project from Toronto, she knew from her China experience she could manage her business remotely. With the promise of enormous sums of money, Rebecca set up a similar system to what she had organized in China. One difference was the larger sum, $100,000, for creating an accident. Half of that would go to the lawyer who referred the client. When the legal system failed to give the wealthy the justice they sought against incompetent doctors, the lawyer would refer them to Rebecca's team.

Their first Toronto client was a wealthy 60-year-old lawyer, Jake Saxman, who suffered after a straightforward rectal operation. There was an anastomotic leak, and the surgeon left him with a permanent colostomy. The incompetence arose because the surgeon failed to act promptly to deal with the complication. The client spent months in the hospital. He was impotent from damage to the sympathetic nerves from the dissection in the pelvis at the time of surgery, as well as permanently disfigured with the colostomy. Jake wanted justice.

After the litigation dragged on for 5 years, the judge finally ruled in favor of the surgeon. The result of the court case was devastating for the client. It convinced him they had rigged the system against the victim, and the only way to get revenge was to use this alternate path. Jake wanted to avenge his pain and suffering when he was in the hospital. He wanted to make the surgeon suffer the same as he did. From the menu of services offered on the dark web, he chose the one that resulted in permanent disfigurement and disability for the surgeon.

This was an especially lucrative client for Rebecca because Jake also wanted revenge against the expert witness, who gave the evidence to support the operating surgeon. Jake felt the expert witness had lied to the judge to protect the operating surgeon. He was happy to pay the $100,000 to have the expert witness meet a fateful accident.

The expert witness who testified in favor of the surgeon in that case was Dr. John Hegland.

Nigel and Rebecca were sipping on their wine as they watched the sun setting in the west. Nigel had calmed down since their argument last week, where they accused each other of sabotaging the business. They now had $200,000 in bitcoin in their internet wallets. Although there was an arrest warrant for him in Canada, he knew they could not arrest him in the Dominican Republic, as there were no extradition treaties between the two countries. How quickly things had turned around for them. Nigel, smiling widely, turned to Rebecca, and they clinked their glasses. "To success!" Nigel cried out.

Chapter 37

John was in his apartment at the kitchen table. After getting kicked out of his house by Marie, he moved to the Hilton Hotel that was down the street from their hospital. He was lucky to find an apartment but had to sign a lease for a year. This brought the tightness in his chest to return, along with the shortness of breath. He recognized that anxiety took over his body because he could not plan for what he would do the next week, let alone a year from now. Nonetheless, he was grateful to find an apartment in such a tight housing market.

Suzie and Marco were sitting with him at the kitchen table. "Ainslie is worried someone will come after me again," John said.

"We are going to stay with you until the danger is over," said Suzie. "It sounds like if something were to happen, it would be within the next week, but it could drag out longer. What did the police say?"

"Sidney Noseworthy gave me the usual spiel about invading privacy and said I was reading too much into it," said John. "He said I needed to calm down. No one is going to come after me again. It is too risky. He conceded he would ask someone to cruise by the apartment during the night for the next week. He said if there is anything I found suspicious, to call him day or night."

The apartment was in downtown Toronto. It was on the ground floor of a three-story building. He had two spare bedrooms, one for each of his children, a small kitchen that opened onto a slightly larger living room, and a single bathroom with a shower. He bought a new Honda SUV with the insurance money from his last car, but only had access to street parking. There was a stone walkway to the front door leading to the three steps to the front door. There was another exit to the apartment through the door in the kitchen, which led to a small backyard. A small barbeque, a wooden table surrounded by four chairs, sat on a concrete stone patio.

"Suzie and I want to hide your car in her underground parking spot in her apartment building," said Marco. We will both park on the street. "I'll drive you to work every morning before I go to my shop."

"The number one cause of death from an accident is automobile crashes," said Suzie. "We'll eliminate that by hiding your car. The next common cause is accidental falls. This is common in those over the age of 65, less so in those younger. Accidental poisoning is another cause. Those three make up the bulk of accidental deaths in Canada."

"What a morbid thing to talk about, "said John. "How about if I hire a security firm to guard me?"

"Most security firms here do not have the training to deal with this," said Marco, "unless they are from a third-world country like Colombia. An assassin would eliminate them before they knew what happened. Your best chance is with me. I know how he would think, having dealt with them in my former life."

"I hate to say this,' said John, "but after all those attempts on my life, wouldn't a prudent assassin try the direct approach with a bullet or knife?"

"Absolutely," said Marco. "We will need to be ready for anything."

John looked at Marco directly into his dark eyes. There was an intensity and determination that John could feel. John felt he could trust those dark, piercing eyes to protect him. "Marco, why are you doing this for me?" asked John. "You made a good life for yourself in Canada. Why risk everything you have built for yourself to help me?"

Marco thought about that for a minute, then replied, "My sister asked me to help. I love my sister. In Colombia, family is everything. I consider you part of my family."

John looked at Suzie, who smiled at him and said, "We are going to take care of you."

Suzie and Marco moved into the spare bedrooms of John's apartment that night after hiding John's car. In the morning, Suzie made breakfast for the three of them. "I'm going to go food shopping tonight," she said. "You have a limited selection of spices. I will make a nice dinner for the three of us tonight."

John smiled. If this was to be his last week on earth before the assassin got to him, to spend it with Suzie would be his only wish. Not only was she beautiful, but he felt safe with her. John thought back to the sailing trip just before Rick set the boat on fire. She was about to kiss him, and he felt powerless to resist. He had not felt like that for a long time. John reflected on Hans' advice about finding red flags before starting a relationship. So far, none came to him when he thought about Suzie. There was a loyalty to him that seemed to emanate from her every pore. The feeling she gave to John was that she would do anything for him. He thought about the picture in Hans' office with the red chairs, and in his mind, Suzie appeared sitting in the chair next to him. She had long red painted nails. They were looking out at the bay at their sailboat.

"John?" asked Suzie. "Are you okay?"

John snapped out of his reverie and said, "Never better. I guess we had better leave." Marco, at the door, was ready to drive him to work.

Marco dropped him at the main entrance of the hospital. "Call me when you are through. I'll pick you up."

John thanked him and watched him drive away. He walked into the hospital as the automatic doors opened and to the operating room. There were four gastric bypasses on his operating room list. The first patient was in the pre-operative area, and he went to see her. The resident, Joel, was there talking to her. "We'll be working together today," Joel said. "We are going to have a great day!"

It was the first time John had worked with Joel, so John showed him the steps in the gastric bypass operation. John's usual approach to teaching the residents was to let them begin with the second case and allow them to go as far as possible. To John's surprise, Joel completed most of the case from start to finish. There were a few areas where Joel struggled, and John took over but handed the operation back to Joel as he was doing an excellent job. Joel had precise movements, and his hands were steady. When he was uncertain what to do next, he would tell John. When John described the next move, Joel would perform it flawlessly, as if he had been doing this type of surgery for a long time.

It was the perfect operating day for John. The resident had a great operative experience. John felt he had provided an excellent learning environment for Joel. The patients received the best possible care. Best of all, they finished operating on time, and the operating room staff were happy to leave on time. On busy days, there would be delays, and they would ask the nurses to stay late, but not today. John called Marco to meet him at the front entrance at 4 pm to drive him home.

"Stay inside the building until I arrive," instructed Marco. "I need to do a few maneuvers to be sure I am not being followed, so I will drive up and stop. Then, I will circle the hospital a few times, looking for a tail. If there are none, I will text you, and you can meet me at the main entrance where I dropped you off this morning."

John received the text. It was okay to meet Marco, so he walked out of the main entrance and into his car. They drove to John's home uneventfully.

"I changed the locks on the doors today," said Marco. He passed a new set of keys to John. John opened the door with the keys, and the smell of exotic spices from cooking overwhelmed his senses. Suzie was standing in front of the stove cooking. "We are having seafood, Paella," said Suzie. "It should be ready in about an hour. You are in for a treat!"

Suzie was right about the food. The classic Spanish dish featured saffron spiced rice, sausage, chicken, and seafood. "In Colombia, we make this better than they do in Valencia, Spain," boasted Suzie.

"This food is truly amazing," said John. "It is the most delicious home-cooked meal I have experienced since when you cooked on the boat."

Suzie smiled and said, "It is my pleasure."

John smiled as well. After dinner and washing the dishes, they talked for a while and discussed their day. Suzie had been at school teaching her grade six students and told a story about two boys who started a fistfight at recess. They were fighting over a girl that they were each trying to impress. The girl confided in Suzie after the fight broke up and they sent the two boys home, that neither of the boys impressed her. Another boy, the one she liked, did not seem to be interested in her. She asked Suzie how she could get his attention. "Do you know what I told her?" asked Suzie. Both John and Marco shook their heads. "Make him a dinner of seafood, Paella. It works every time!" John and Marco laughed.

They went to their separate rooms for the night, and John fell asleep within minutes of laying his head on the pillow.

John woke up to a ping coming from his phone. He saw there was a text message. It was from Ainslie. "Dad, I had a huge fight with mom. I am at the front door and cannot get in. Did you change the locks?"

John sighed. Ainslie could usually avoid confrontations with her mother. Often, she would ignore her, but sometimes, her mother would push some buttons that would send Ainslie into a rage. To come here at 2 AM must have been a serious fight between them. John went to the front door and opened it.

Instead of Ainslie standing in front of him was Remo, the brother of Rick. He was almost as large as Rick and had a lop-sided grin on his face. His piercing dark eyes were the same as Rick's. He was standing with a baton in his hand, smacking it with a thud. He stared at John, who stood frozen in position. Remo did not say a word but kept smacking the baton.

John looked past Remo, expecting to see Ainslie. Laying on the stone walkway leading to the house was Marco. He was not moving. John could not tell if he was unconscious or dead.

"Where's my daughter, Ainslie!" John shouted. "You bastard! What have you done with her?"

Remo was quiet for a few seconds and kept smacking the baton. "The last I saw her; she was sleeping in her bed. That's how

I got her phone. You need a better security system in your house. Yours is too easy to disarm."

John tried to shut the door, but Remo's foot prevented it from closing. The door flew open, and the baton in Remo's hand cracked across his face. John fell to the floor. After a few minutes, he woke up. He was sitting in a chair in the backyard. Duct tape pinning his legs to the chair prevented him from getting up. Remo had stuffed a rag in his mouth and taped it shut. His hands, taped to the edge of the table so only the fingers were showing, prevented any movement.

"My brother died a painful death thanks to you," said Remo. "Jack, the police officer in Antigua, told me there was not much left of him after you fed him to the sharks. They ate him piece by piece. The same is going to happen to you tonight. Only I am going to start with your fingers. As a surgeon, they must be a valuable part of your anatomy. I am going to work my way and take off your arms and, if you are still alive, your legs. I'll leave you to bleed to death after that. I have been looking forward to this for months. I would have done this for free, but the $20,000 they paid me makes it even more enjoyable."

Remo pulled out a butcher's knife and, in less than 3 seconds, chopped off the 5th finger from John's right hand. John let out a blood-curdling scream that was almost completely muzzled by the rag stuffed in his mouth. The pain was intense, and he could feel tears streaming down the sides of his face. He could not move and only could wiggle. He could hear his muzzled screams as he watched the digital artery pump blood in an arch to the far side of the table.

John watched with his eyes so wide they felt they would pop out of his head as Remo raised the butcher's knife to slice off the next finger. The scream came out as a muzzled sound. John closed his eyes and waited for the inevitable. Nothing happened. After 15 seconds, he opened his eyes. Remo was lying on the ground with the claws of a hammer sticking out of his head. Suzie was standing over him, hyperventilating.

Things happened quickly after that. The ambulance arrived at the same time as Sidney Noseworthy. The ambulance staff instructed Suzie to put the severed finger into a baggy and then into a bag of ice for transport to the hospital. Sidney asked a few questions and said there would be a more detailed interview later. They loaded John into an ambulance. Suzie hopped in and sat beside him on the stretcher. The lights and sirens were on full as the ambulance raced to the closest emergency room.

Marco was alive but unconscious. The ambulance transported him to a neurosurgery unit. Suzie explained to John while they were transporting him to the hospital that they were taking shifts watching the apartment from the outside. Remo must have belted Marco with the club, knocking him out. Suzie was to relieve him at 2 AM and that is when she saw John strapped to the chair and table through the kitchen window at the back.

"The hammer was the closest weapon," she explained. "It took all my concentration to stay quiet while I got close enough to bury the claws of the hammer into his skull. There were tears in my eyes as I saw him lift the butcher's knife to slice off another finger. It petrified me. I worried I would cry out, and he would turn around and stop me. I hate to think of the outcome."

They arrived at the hospital, and the paramedics wheeled John into the emergency room. Within one hour, John was in the operating room to reattach his severed finger.

When John woke up the morning after the surgery, he recognized he was in a room at the hospital. He looked at the bandage around the reattached finger. The tip of the finger was open to the bandage, and the skin was pink. The surgery was a success, thought John. There was no feeling at the tip of the finger. Nerves grow at an inch per month, so it might take three months to get a feeling there. Physiotherapy would get the movement back to a functioning level in six months.

Suzie was sleeping in the folding chair in the room's corner. She breathed quietly and curled her body in the fetal position. She looked like she was at peace, lying there in the dim light of the morning. A lock of her curly hair partially covered her face. A white hospital blanket covered her and moved up and down as she breathed. John stared at her. He smiled as he thought about how she saved his life. What a stark contrast to Marie, he thought.

There was a knock at the door. Marco walked in. He surveyed the room with his eyes as if looking for danger. Opening the bathroom door, he glanced inside, and finding nothing that concerned him, he looked at Suzie, sleeping peacefully. He sat on the edge of John's bed. "Are you OK?" he asked with a worried look.

"You and Suzie saved my life," said John. "They reattached my finger last night. It would have been much worse if Suzie had not been so handy with a hammer." John told him what had happened.

"I was watching the apartment from behind the hedge in your neighbor's yard," said Marco. "I saw him approach the house. I am skilled at hand-to-hand combat from my training in Colombia, but he surprised me with the club. I'm sorry I failed you." Marco looked down at his hands. "I can't believe he did that."

"Look," said John, "the guy is a psychopath. Sidney told me that Rick and Remo would start bar fights for fun and leave their opponents permanently crippled. Imagine how guilty I would feel if that had happened to you. You need to remember you were giving me the biggest gift any human could give to another. You were taking care of me. Thank you." John sat up in the bed and gave a hug to Marco.

Suzie was awake by now and was watching the men. She walked over and joined the hug. "I'll go to Starbucks and get us some coffee," said Marco as he disengaged from the hug.

Suzie was sitting on the edge of the bed, looking down at John. "Suzie," said John, looking directly into her soft brown eyes.

Suzie put her finger on his lips. "I know how you feel about me," she whispered. "One thing you need to know about us Latin women. When we choose a man, we stay with him through whatever life throws at him. Compared to you, North Americans, we take commitment to a new level. I am going to take care of you forever. This is just the beginning of a new life for us."

John smiled at her. He felt at peace for the first time in a very long time.

Chapter 38

Using a telescopic lens, he could see them sitting on the veranda drinking wine. It was dusk, but he could see them both clearly. They were sitting down. The distance was 600 feet across the bay, a sure shot for him. He lined up the woman in his sights. Aiming for the right temple, the thinnest part of the skull, he pulled the trigger. A second later, she toppled over. The telescopic lens lined up the man in the same part of his skull before he had time to react to the woman falling over. He pulled the trigger, and the man fell to the veranda floor.

He surveyed the veranda for a full minute with the telescopic lens and saw no movement. He placed his gun in a traveling case and closed it. There was no way he was going to let amateurs move in on the business he had created over the last 5 years. A serious talk with the lawyer who sent the business to a competitor would happen when he returned to Toronto. This lawyer would not make the same mistake again.

The sniper handed the gun case to his assistant. She would send it by courier to their warehouse in Toronto. She drove him to the private airport near Samana. Sidney Noseworthy then climbed aboard the private jet for the flight back to Toronto.

The End

www.ingramcontent.com/pod-product-compliance
Lightning Source LLC
Chambersburg PA
CBHW070634310726

48982CB00001B/280